THE LOVE OF GOLF

Consultant:
David Barrett

Publications International, Ltd.

David Barrett was an editor at *Golf Magazine* for 18 years. He is the author of *Golf Rules Explained* and a contributing writer to *Best of Golf, 20th Century Golf Chronicle, Golf Legends of All Time, Wit & Wisdom of Golf*, and *Golf in America: The First One Hundred Years.*

Contributing Writers: Al Barkow, David Barrett, Peter Blais, David Earl, Rhonda Glenn, Bob Harig, Ken Janke, and Pat Seelig.

Louis Weber, CEO
Publications International, Ltd.
7373 North Cicero Avenue
Lincolnwood, Illinois 60712

Manufactured in China.

8 7 6 5 4 3 2 1

ISBN-13: 978-1-4127-1132-6
ISBN-10: 1-4127-1132-0

Library of Congress Control Number: 2004115109

Contents

Chapter One

Old-Timers and All-Timers:

Legends of Golf

Played for centuries, this is a game of proud traditions and rich heritage. Memories are long, and the immortals easily recalled.

Ted Ray tees off at Scotland's Royal and Ancient Golf Club of St. Andrews.

Ben Hogan

For the first eight years of Ben Hogan's career, his driving featured a wild hook. But he took practicing to an extraordinary level for golfers of his era and was an inquisitive student of the golf swing. Henry Picard, a Masters and PGA champion in the 1930s, convinced Hogan to "weaken" his left-hand grip by turning the hand more to the left. Seemingly overnight, Hogan's basic shot became a left-to-right power fade, a trajectory that came to be known as the "Hogan Fade."

Hogan's career took off. From 1940 to 1942, he won 15 tournaments and was the Tour's leading money winner. After an interruption for service during World War II, he picked up where he'd left off. From 1946 through early 1949, playing what he described as the best golf of his life, he won 32 tournaments, including his first three majors—the 1946 and 1948 PGA Championships and the 1948 U.S. Open.

Hogan was sidelined the next year by a life-threatening auto accident, but displaying impressive strength and determination, he returned in 1950 to win the U.S. Open. Even after cutting his schedule back to preserve his strength, Hogan still won five more major championships—two U.S. Opens, two Masters, and one British Open. In 1953, he won what might be called golf's Triple Crown—the U.S. and British Opens and the Masters.

***In addition to his playing career, Hogan founded a hugely successful golf equipment company and produced a best-selling sports book,* Five Lessons: The Modern Fundamentals of Golf.**

"One of the greatest pleasures in golf—I can think of nothing that truly compares with it unless it is watching a well-played shot streak for the flag—is the sensation a golfer experiences at the instant he contacts the ball flush and correctly."

—Ben Hogan,
Five Lessons: The Modern Fundamentals of Golf

"Golf is a day spent in a round of strenuous idleness."

—William Wordsworth

"The difference between now and when I played during my younger days is my drives are shorter and my short game is longer."

—Simon Hobday

Major Professional Championship Breakdown

	British Open	U.S. Open	PGA Champ.	Masters	Total
Jack Nicklaus	3	4	5	6	18
Tiger Woods	3	2	3	4	12
Walter Hagen	4	2	5	0	11
Ben Hogan	1	4	2	2	9
Gary Player	3	1	2	3	9
Tom Watson	5	1	0	2	8
Bobby Jones	3	4	0	0	7
Arnold Palmer	2	1	0	4	7
Gene Sarazen	1	2	3	1	7
Sam Snead	1	0	3	3	7
Harry Vardon	6	1	0	0	7
Nick Faldo	3	0	0	3	6
Lee Trevino	2	2	2	0	6

Jones Wins Grand Slam

It wasn't entirely unthinkable that in one year Bobby Jones could win the four major championships of his era—the U.S. and British Amateurs and Opens. Early in 1930, Bobby Cruickshank predicted it, bet on it, and won a large sum of money.

Jones's most anxious moment in the British Amateur at St. Andrews was in the fourth round, when Cyril Tolley had a 12-foot birdie putt on the last hole to win 1 up. He missed, and Jones won on the first extra hole after laying a stymie on his foe. At Hoylake two weeks later, Jones led the British Open through the first three rounds and broke the 72-hole course record by 10 strokes.

On to Minnesota and the U.S. Open, the third leg. At the Interlachen Country Club, Jones took a five-shot lead with a third-round 68—the lowest he ever shot in this, his 11th and last U.S. Open. Nevertheless, he had to birdie three of the last six holes in the final round to win by two over Macdonald Smith. A 40-foot birdie putt on the last green was the clincher.

Given his own momentum, and the undoubted awe everyone had by the time the U.S. Amateur came around, his victory in that championship was practically assured. Jones won the 36-hole qualifying medal at Merion Cricket Club in Pennsylvania with 69–73. In the matches, he was never down to any opponent. Jones then retired for all time from championship golf. He was just 28 years old.

George Trevor, in The New York Sun, *called Jones's feat "the Impregnable Quadrilateral." No one before or since has won all four championships in one year, and with the Opens now dominated by pros, it's unthinkable that anyone ever will. Jones appears here on the right.*

"Golf is *20 percent* mechanics and technique. The other *80 percent* is philosophy, humor, tragedy, romance, melodrama, companionship, cussedness, and conversation."

—Grantland Rice

The "Church Pew" of Oakmont

William and Henry Fownes completed their famous Oakmont Country Club course in 1903. Set atop a hill north of Pittsburgh, the course quickly became known for its difficulty. Greens were super slick and heavily contoured. Oakmont's most famous feature remains the "church pew" bunker, which lies between the third and fourth fairways.

ERGENCY
AID STATION

Gene Sarazen

In 1922, 20-year-old Gene Sarazen surprised everyone except himself by winning the U.S. Open with the kind of verve, nerve, and brass that characterized his personality and golf game for the next 30 years. On the last hole, he was deep in contention and had a crucial decision to make.

"I hit a good drive," he said, "and for my second there was water to the left and out-of-bounds on the right. My caddie wanted me to play safe, but I heard somebody say [Bobby] Jones and [Bill] Mehlhorn were doing well [a few holes back]. So I said, 'Oh, hell. Give me that brassie.' I shot right for the green and put it about 12 feet from the cup." Sarazen putted for a birdie and won by a stroke. Later that year, he won the PGA Championship. Sarazen was indeed on his way.

By winning the 1935 Masters, Sarazen became the first player to win all four tournaments that would later make up the Grand Slam events: the Masters, U.S. Open, British Open, and PGA Championship.

Palmer Charges to Win Masters, U.S. Open

Arnold Palmer vaulted into the spotlight in 1960 as a player of near-mythic proportion. Like a knight charging after the holy grail, Palmer galloped to final-round surges to win his second Masters and his only U.S. Open.

In April, Palmer badly wanted to regain the Masters title he had first claimed in 1958. He played brilliantly but was one stroke behind Ken Venturi at the third round's 16th hole. Squinting into the setting sun, Palmer mounted his now-famous "charge." He birdied the last two holes and won the tournament by a stroke.

At June's U.S. Open, played at Cherry Hills Country Club in Denver, Palmer was in trouble from the start. He tried to drive the green of the 1st hole, a downhill par-4 of 346 yards, but drove into a hazard and made a double bogey. At the end of the third round on Saturday, Palmer trailed Mike Souchak by seven strokes. More than a dozen players were ahead of Arnie.

At lunch before the final round, he asked, "I may shoot 65. What would that do?" "Nothing," said golf writer Bob Drum. "You're too far back." "The hell I am," Palmer snapped. "A 65 would give me 280, and 280 wins Opens."

Palmer tried to drive the 1st green again, hitting a smoking tee shot, and his ball bounded through a belt of rough fronting the green and rolled onto the putting surface 20 feet from the hole. He nearly holed his eagle putt, and he made his birdie. Birdieing the next three holes, Palmer was only three strokes behind Souchak. Galleries raced to Palmer's side. He also birdied the 6th and 7th and made the turn in 30 strokes.

Souchak faltered, while Palmer remained steady on the back nine. He holed his last par putt for a 65 and the 280 he had wanted. When the winning putt fell, Palmer flung his white visor high into the air. It was a spectacular victory for the PGA Tour's most charismatic star.

17 18
4 4
2 2
4 5
1 1
0 0
1 0
1 1
0 1
LEGEND
Red Figures - Under Par
Green Zero - Even Par
Green Figures Over Par
Scores As Shown Are
On A Cumulative Basis
CLAUDE
HAWKINS - 69
SOUCHAK 34 OUT
FINSTERWALD

"The *only way* of really finding out a *man's* true character is to play *golf* with him."

—P. G. Wodehouse

A Whole Different Ballgame

Baseball's Ted Williams and golf's Sam Snead once got into a discussion about which game was harder to play. Williams took the lead, pointing out that in golf the ball, although small, isn't moving and you hit it off a flat surface. In baseball, he said, "I gotta stand up there with a round bat and hit a ball that's traveling at me at around a hundred miles an hour, and curving."

Snead considered that for a moment, then responded: "Yeah, Ted, but you don't have to go up in the stands and play your foul balls. Golfers do."

Sam Snead

Snead won his first tournament as a professional in 1936. He won his last on the regular PGA Tour, the Greater Greensboro Open, in 1965, just short of his 53rd birthday, making him the oldest winner ever on the Tour.

Although he won a record 82 tournaments on the PGA Tour, including three Masters, three PGA Championships, and one British Open, he never won the U.S. Open.

In the three times Snead faced Ben Hogan in a head-to-head playoff—including once for the Masters—he won every time.

Snead won the granddaddy of tournaments, the British Open, on the grandest course, St. Andrews, prevailing by a full four strokes in 1946.

"Watching Sam Snead practice hitting golf balls is like watching a fish practice swimming."

—Former pro John Schlee

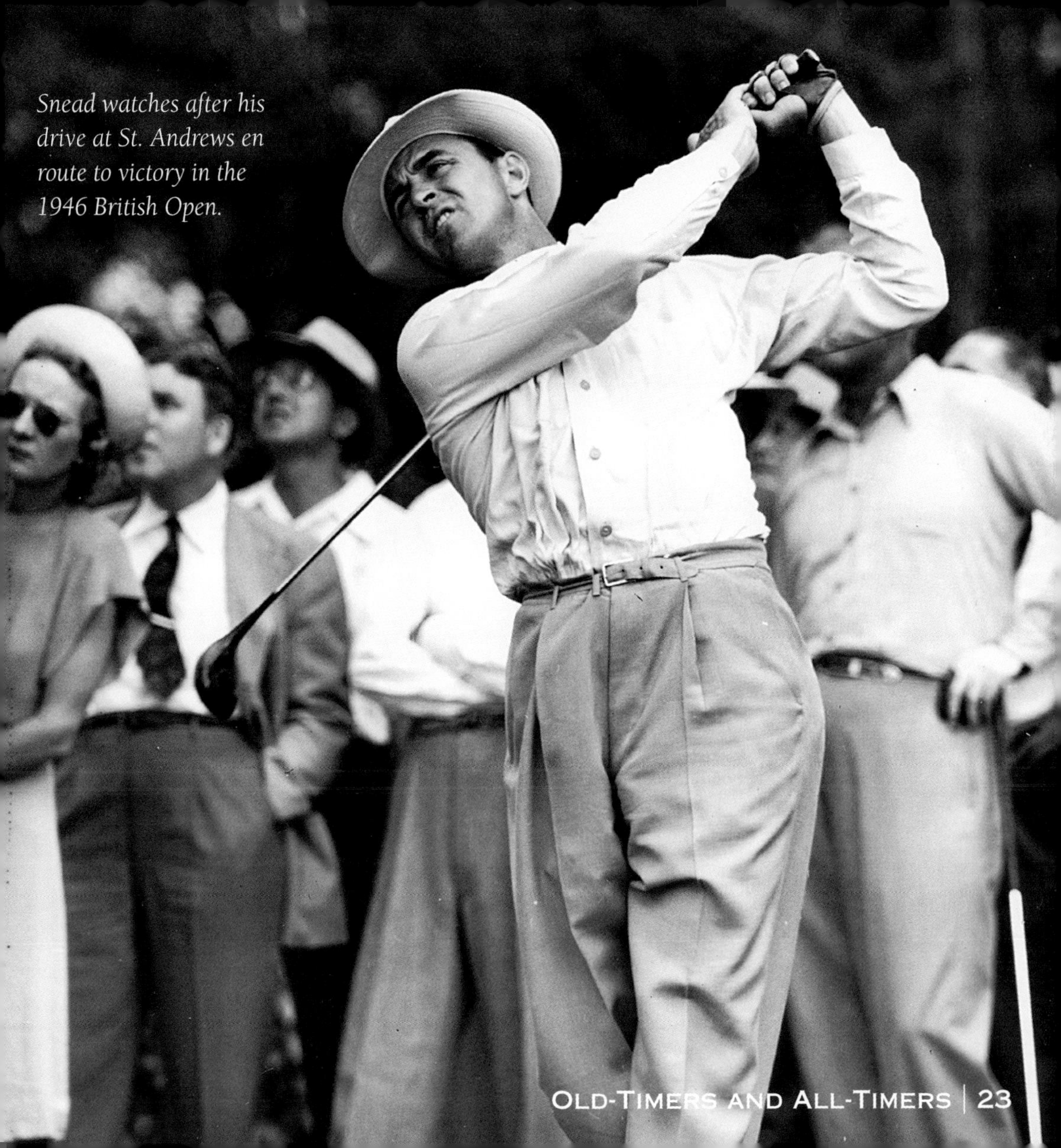

Snead watches after his drive at St. Andrews en route to victory in the 1946 British Open.

Asked in the mid-1970s to list the ten greatest golfers of all time, Sam Snead provided the following ranking:

1. ____________
2. Jack Nicklaus
3. Ben Hogan
4. Byron Nelson
5. Arnold Palmer
6. Bobby Jones
7. Walter Hagen
8. Gene Sarazen
9. Billy Casper
10. Gary Player

When asked why he didn't name someone No. 1, Snead replied, "I might have made a lot of enemies." Only Sam knows if he would have placed his own name in that position.

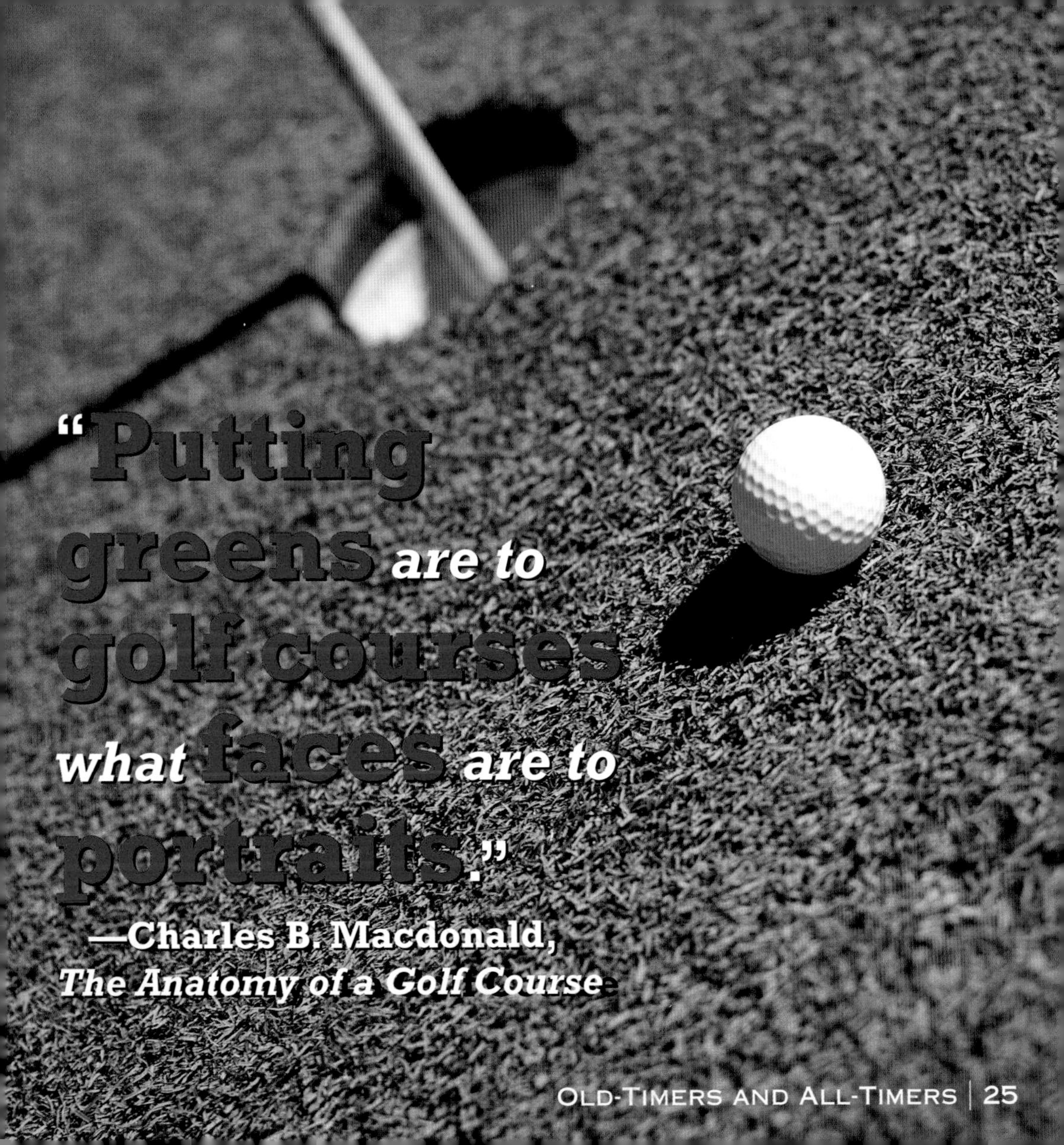

"Putting greens are to golf courses what faces are to portraits."

—Charles B. Macdonald, *The Anatomy of a Golf Course*

Pebble Beach

Pebble Beach Golf Links features nine holes playing directly along the water's edge. Holes 6 through 10 dance along the cliffs. The 7th is considered one of the world's best par-3s. The 8th is a knee-buckling par-4 with a blind tee shot to the edge of a cliff. The approach is a spectacular 190 yards downhill over a gaping chasm to a postage-stamp green, which is protected by three traps and deep rough.

The par-3, 209-yard 17th plays into the prevailing ocean breeze to an hourglass green backed by sand, rocks, and the Pacific. A breathtaking view of the shoreline stretches the length of the par-5, 548-yard 18th. It leads to a green partially blocked on the right by trees and flanked on three sides by bunkers.

The 107-yard 7th hole plays downhill to a green that reaches into Carmel Bay. The wind blew so hard during the 1960 Crosby National Pro-Am that winner Ken Venturi used a 3-iron to reach the hole.

Zaharias Beats Cancer, Wins U.S. Open

Babe Zaharias, the great athlete and larger-than-life personality, announced in January 1954 that she would play the LPGA's full schedule. This was no small news. Babe had undergone surgery for colon cancer the previous April and had missed the rest of the 1953 season. Without its biggest gate attraction, the women's tour was starved for publicity. Babe's return would guarantee revived interest in the LPGA.

Babe's running conversation with galleries and cocky exuberance had made her the LPGA's top drawing card, and interest in her return was great. Gaining strength through her first few events, Babe won the Miami Women's Open and the Sarasota Women's Open back-to-back. "I feel wonderful," she said. "I think I'm here to stay."

Babe set her sights on the U.S. Women's Open, which she had won in 1948 and 1950. She jumped to a six-stroke lead after opening 72–71. However, Babe and the other players knew that Saturday's double round would severely test her endurance.

On a mild, cloudless day, Babe fired a 73 in the morning and had a 10-stroke lead. She rested between rounds, but late in the afternoon, Babe began to tire. She started pushing her tee shots and bogied four holes coming in. In the end it didn't matter, as she won by a whopping 12 strokes. Approaching the final green, she was nearly mobbed by well-wishers.

At the presentation ceremony, Babe was subdued. "My prayers have been answered," she said. "I wanted to show thousands of cancer sufferers that the operation I had, colostomy, will enable a person to return to normal life. . . . This is my answer to them."

Two years later, she lost her battle with cancer. An irrepressible personality and great champion, Babe Zaharias drew attention to women's golf in a day when few people cared to watch. Today, she is remembered as America's first female sports hero.

After major cancer surgery, Zaharias returned to the LPGA Tour with her doctor's blessings. Weakened by the disease, she started 1954 slowly, but victories in February and May meant that Babe was back. When she endured Saturday's double round to win the 1954 U.S. Women's Open, Babe capped off one of golf's most dramatic comeback stories.

Best Rounds

Henry Cotton shattered the 18-hole record at the British Open with a 65 in the second round in 1934 at Royal St. George's. The round was so good that a ball was named after it, the Dunlop 65.

Robert Trent Jones's redesign of Oakland Hills before the 1951 U.S. Open resulted in the nickname of "The Monster." Through three rounds, no player broke 70, but **Ben Hogan** solved the riddle of the course with a 67 in the final round.

After two rounds of the 1965 Masters, **Jack Nicklaus** was tied with Arnold Palmer and Gary Player for the lead. Nicklaus blew them away with a 64 in the third round, tying the course record on the way to a nine-stroke victory.

Johnny Miller entered the final round of the 1973 U.S. Open six strokes out of the lead, but he stole the title with the greatest round in Open history, an 8-under-par 63 at Oakmont in Pennsylvania.

In the second round of the 1977 Danny Thomas Memphis Classic, **Al Geiberger** shot a 59, becoming the first player to break 60 on the PGA Tour.

Gary Player was barely in the picture going into the final round of the 1978 Masters, trailing by seven strokes. But with birdies on seven of the last ten holes, the South African reeled off a closing 64 to claim his third green jacket.

Of the 20 times that a 63 has been shot in a major championship, **Greg Norman** did it in probably the toughest conditions on the way to winning the 1986 British Open at Turnberry.

It's one thing to shoot a 59 on the PGA Tour, but to do it in the final round to win a tournament by one

Sandwich Club Captain Hon. Michael Scott congratulates Harry Cotton in 1934.

stroke is the ultimate in drama. That's what **David Duval** pulled off in the 1999 Bob Hope Chrysler Classic, where he trailed by seven strokes entering the final round.

Tiger Woods had probably the greatest year ever in golf in 2000, and his best round came in the second round of the WGC-NEC Invitational, where he shot a 61 at Firestone Country Club in Ohio.

Chauvinists believed no woman would ever crack 60 on the LPGA Tour. At the 2001 Standard Register PING, **Annika Sorenstam** proved them wrong, shooting a 59. "I'm overwhelmed," she said. "I can't believe what I just did."

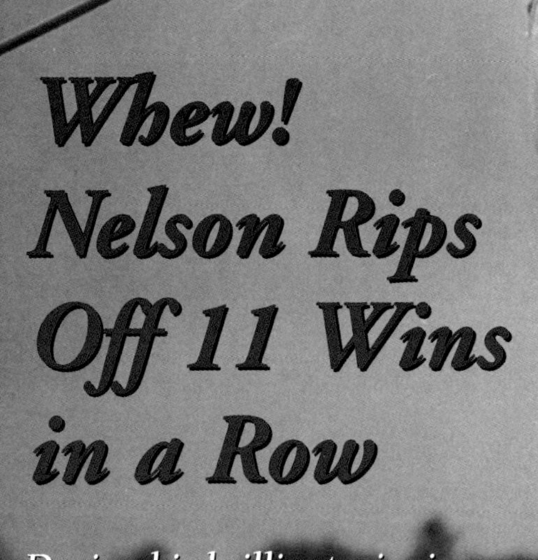

Whew! Nelson Rips Off 11 Wins in a Row

During his brilliant winning streak, Byron Nelson played 38 rounds of straight stroke play at 113-under-par, averaging 67.92 strokes per round.

Byron Nelson set a standard of excellence that goes beyond mere dominance of a sport. How does one describe a golfer who, in one year, 1945, wins 18 official tournaments—11 of them in a row?

The Streak was the feature story. It began in March when Nelson and his partner, Jug McSpaden, won the Miami International 4-Ball. After that, Nelson was on his own. The second straight win was a close one. In the Charlotte Open, Nelson needed a blistering 33 in the final nine just to tie Sam Snead. He got it, and the two also tied in the playoff, with the lead changing hands four times. In the second playoff, Nelson won by four with a 69.

From then on, Nelson made every effort to avoid close calls, often by making inspired rushes of brilliant golf in the closing rounds—streaks within The Streak. Nelson's second-round match in the PGA Championship was his toughest. He was two down with four holes to go against Mike Turnesa, but he went 4-under-par with two birdies and an eagle to win, 1 up.

Nelson would one day admit that the competition was not as tough as it might have been. Snead played in all but three events of The Streak, but in a few he was recovering from a broken wrist. Ben Hogan and Jimmy Demaret competed in only two each. Other young stars who were also in the military at the time played perhaps two each. Yet one must not downplay the brilliance of Byron's play. In 38 rounds at straight stroke play, Nelson was 113-under-par, averaging 67.92 per round.

Ironically, his streak ended when an amateur, Freddie Haas, Jr., won the Memphis Open. Nelson was third. Nelson played only one more year of full-time tournament golf, retiring after a six-victory campaign in 1946, even though he was only 34. His sustained excellence may well have worn him out. Ultimately, he would suggest as much.

"However unlucky you may be, it really is unfair to expect your adversary's grief for your undeserved misfortunes to be as poignant as your own."

—Horace Hutchinson

Is That an Oil Painting?

Tommy Bolt was famous for his temper on the golf course. It was sometimes volatile, other times a subtle expression of his displeasure. A famous example of the latter was the time Bolt was playing in the first round of a Tour event at the Whitemarsh Country Club in Philadelphia. On a par-3 with a two-level green and the pin cut on the back (upper) portion, Bolt hit a wonderful tee shot that landed on the lower level and jumped up to within a foot of the hole.

This brilliant display of shot-making received not a sound of recognition from the sizable gallery behind the green, a nonresponse that prompted Bolt to say to his caddie, "Son, I know I can't see very well anymore, but my hearing is still okay. Tell me, is that an oil painting of people behind that green?" When told it was a live audience, Bolt replied, "Well, if those folks don't appreciate the shot I just hit up there, old Tom Bolt is not playing here anymore." With that, Bolt withdrew from the tournament.

Mickey Wright

As an amateur on the national level, Wright won the 1952 U.S. Girls' Junior and the 1954 World Amateur. She was also the low amateur in the 1954 U.S. Women's Open.

At 23, she led after every round of the 1958 U.S. Open, setting a new Open scoring record with a 2-under-par 290.

Wright is second in all-time LPGA victories with 82. She won three majors in one season—the 1961 U.S. Women's Open, LPGA, and Titleholders.

Winning 13 times in 1963, she set a stratospheric record in the Byron Nelson class that many feel will never be equaled.

Wright took a golf class in college. Final grade: D.

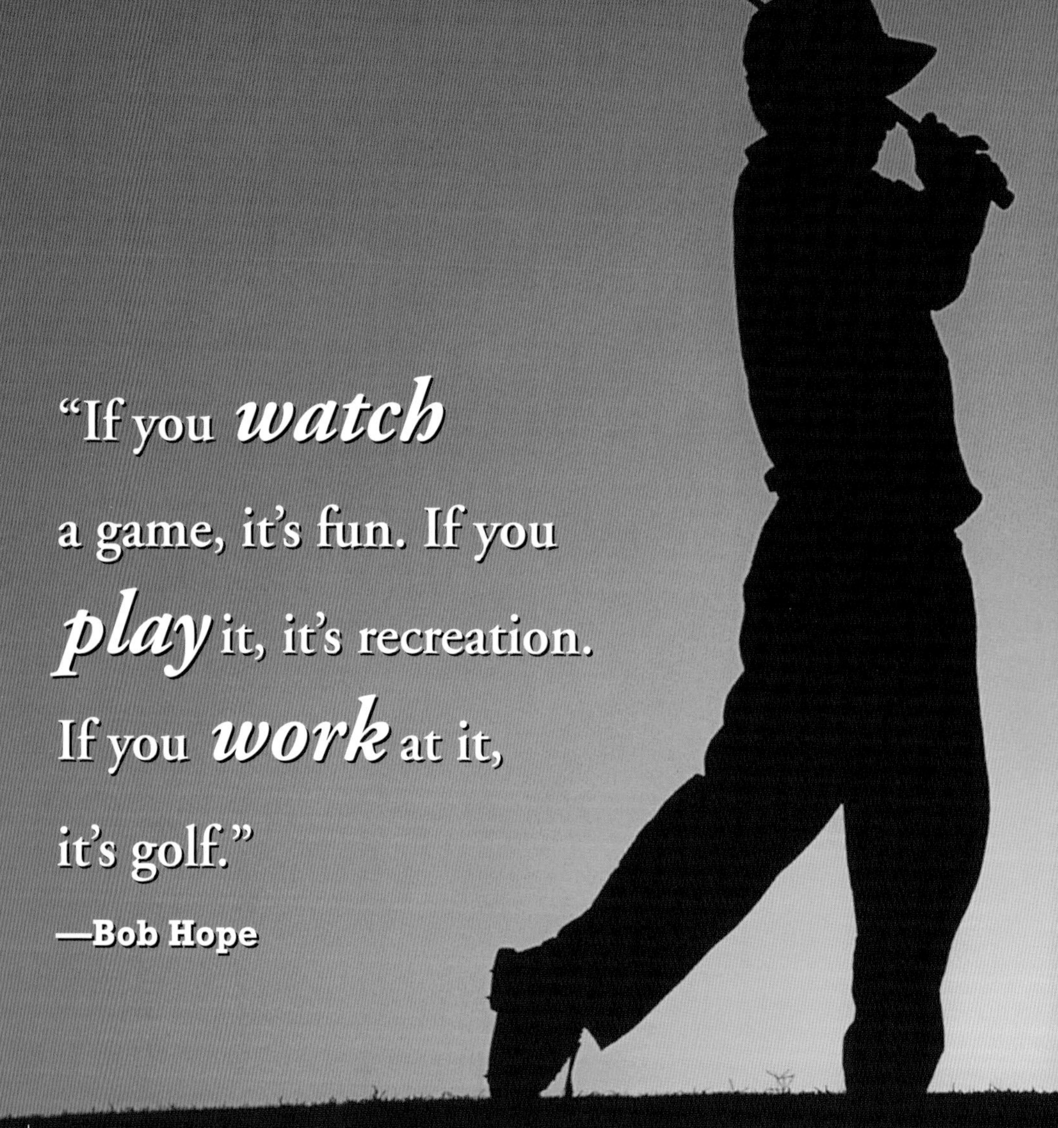

"If you *watch* a game, it's fun. If you *play* it, it's recreation. If you *work* at it, it's golf."

—Bob Hope

"Unlike the other Scottish game of whiskey-drinking, excess in golf is not injurious to the health."

—Sir Walter Simpson

Shinnecock Hills

Shinnecock Hills, completed in 1891, was the first 18-hole course in America and the first U.S. course to import a professional designer to undertake its layout. Scotsman Willie Dunn came to America at the behest of a rich New York business syndicate. Dunn originally developed 12 holes for the course. Later, he added a women's nine-hole layout that was eventually incorporated into the original design to make a full 18.

Charles Macdonald in 1916 and William Flynn in 1931 later revised the layout and are generally credited with giving the course, which sits on an expansive 200 acres, its current flavor. Shinnecock, along with St. Andrews, Newport Country Club, Chicago Golf Club, and The Country Club at Brookline, formed the Amateur Golf Association in 1894, which later became the United States Golf Association (USGA).

The holes wander back and forth over the property. Consequently, the wind, which blows most of the time, is always attacking from a different direction, forcing golfers to continuously think about their game and use most every club in their bag. Holes that usually play downwind tend to be longer but receptive to bump-and-run approaches. Holes playing into the wind are generally shorter. The wind, tall grasses, and seaside location give the course a distinctly Scottish feel and make it play much longer than its 6,813-yard length. Water comes into play on a single hole.

Shinnecock boasts the oldest clubhouse in the United States, a Stanford White design that looks out over much of the course from its perch behind the 9th green.

Nelson Nips Snead to Claim PGA Championship

Sam Snead (*left*) and Byron Nelson (*right*) hoisted the winner's trophy before the last round of the 1940 PGA Championship at Hershey Country Club in Pennsylvania. In a thriller, Nelson finished 1 up over Snead. Nelson's victory made up for the previous year, when he lost to Henry Picard in the PGA final.

Nicklaus Better Than the Pros in U.S. Open

Arnold Palmer *(left)* and amateur Jack Nicklaus *(right)* finished one-two in the 1960 U.S. Open. The young Nicklaus, reigning U.S. Amateur champion, beat every pro except Palmer to win the silver medal. Palmer fired a winning total of 280 to Nicklaus's 282. It was the best showing by an amateur since 1933, when Johnny Goodman won.

When You're Hot, You're Hot

Byron Nelson
11 straight victories, 1945

Lawson Little
U.S. and British Amateurs, 1934–1935

Tiger Woods
six straight wins, 1999–2000; five straight, 2006

Lee Trevino
three wins—U.S. Open, Canadian Open, British Open, 1971

Ben Hogan
six straight wins, 1948

Nancy Lopez
five straight victories, 1978

Annika Sorenstam
five straight victories, 2004–2005

Mickey Wright
one streak of four, another of three, 1963

Lawson Little (center) *captured the 1934 and 1935 U.S. and British Amateurs, defeating 29 challengers in all.*

Bobby Jones
Grand Slam—U.S. and British Opens and U.S. and British Amateurs, 1930

Hale Irwin
16 victories, 1997–1998 on Champions PGA Tour

"IF YOU'RE PLAYING WELL, THEY COULD PROBABLY PUT THE PIN ON THE CART PATH AND YOU COULD GET IT CLOSE."

—*Mike Sullivan*

"There are two kinds of golf—golf and tournament golf. They are not the same."

—Bobby Jones

TIGHT SECURITY

During the 1926 British Open, Bobby Jones forgot his badge that enabled him to enter the grounds so he could compete. He tried to get through the gate, but an official turned him away. Jones simply went to the public entrance and bought a ticket. Of course, he won the championship.

Jones is pictured at the 1930 British Open at Hoylake.

Glenna Collett Vare

A contemporary of Bobby Jones, Glenna Collett Vare dominated women's amateur golf in the United States much the same way Jones did the men's game. Her enduring legacy is a record six U.S. Women's Amateur titles—this in a time when women's professional golf didn't exist.

Vare was perhaps the longest hitter women's golf had ever seen. Asked later how she was able to outdrive her contemporaries, she said, "Very simple. I just hit the ball harder than they did." Collett won her first Women's Amateur in 1922 and claimed her second title in 1925.

In 1928, Collett began a streak that saw her win 19 consecutive matches in the U.S. Women's Amateur, carrying her to titles in 1928, 1929, and 1930. After marrying in 1931, she won her sixth Women's Amateur in 1935.

The one big title she never claimed was the Ladies' British Open Amateur, in which she reached the final twice, losing to Joyce Wethered in 1929 and Diana Fishwick in 1930.

"The man who can putt is a match for anyone."

—Willie Park, Jr.

Sarazen Plays Par-5 Hole in Two, Wins Masters

On the last day of play in the 1935 Masters, Gene Sarazen came to the 15th hole of the Augusta National Golf Club as the only player with any chance of catching Craig Wood, who was finishing a round of 282.

At the tee of the 485-yard par-5 15th, Sarazen drove the ball well, some 250 yards into the right side of the fairway. Sarazen—who made popular the phrase "miss 'em quick"—wasted no time over the ball. But he didn't miss. A double eagle! With one swing of the club, he'd made up his entire deficit. He parred the remaining three holes to tie Wood.

Wood, according to one reporter, "looked like a man who had won a sweepstakes and then had lost the ticket on the way to the payoff window." Sarazen continued his winning ways in the next day's playoff.

Gene Sarazen (left) *receives congratulations from runner-up Craig Wood after winning the 1935 Masters.*

St. Andrews

Despite the efforts of people and nature to alter its linksland appearance, the Old Course at St. Andrews would likely be recognized by those who first played the game there hundreds of years ago.

Golf was a popular sport among the locals when the country's oldest university was founded on Scotland's east coast in 1413. In fact, the game was such a distraction that King James II banned it in 1457 by an act of the Scottish Parliament because archers were spending more time practicing with their clubs than their bows.

In 1754 local hackers founded the Society of St. Andrews Golfers, later renamed the Royal and Ancient Golf Club, golf's governing body throughout much of the world.

Despite its reputation as the Home of Golf, the Old Course at St. Andrews is an acquired taste. Unseen bunkers—with such names as Hell and Ginger Beer—wreak havoc on the first-time visitor's game while eliciting a knowing smile from the Old Course veteran.

The legends of the game have passed over the stone bridge on the 18th hole in search of championships, knowledge, and inspiration.

PATTY WHO SHOT 122?

Patty Berg became one of the all-time best women golfers, but her career might not have developed at all if not for a magical moment when she was just a beginner. She recalled that seminal event years later:

> Winning the 1934 Minneapolis City Ladies Championship was the most memorable event in my golf career, because I probably wouldn't have had a golf career if not for what happened. I played in my first City Ladies Championship the year before, when I was 15, and shot 122. . . . I walked back to the clubhouse and said to myself, I'm going to spend the next 365 days trying to improve. For the next year, all I did was eat, sleep, and play golf. It was worth every freckle on my face, because 365 days later I was medalist and won the Minneapolis City Ladies title.
>
> I didn't think I'd win that tournament. When I did, I started to dream . . . that golf was my future, and that's exactly how it turned out.

LPGA Annual Money Leaders

Year	Player	Earnings
1950	Babe Zaharias	$14,800
1951	Babe Zaharias	$15,087
1952	Betsy Rawls	$14,505
1953	Louise Suggs	$19,816
1954	Patty Berg	$16,011
1955	Patty Berg	$16,492
1956	Marlene Hagge	$20,235
1957	Patty Berg	$16,272
1958	Beverly Hanson	$12,639
1959	Betsy Rawls	$26,774
1960	Louise Suggs	$16,892
1961	Mickey Wright	$22,236
1962	Mickey Wright	$21,641
1963	Mickey Wright	$31,269
1964	Mickey Wright	$29,800
1965	Kathy Whitworth	$28,658
1966	Kathy Whitworth	$33,517
1967	Kathy Whitworth	$32,937
1968	Kathy Whitworth	$48,379
1969	Carol Mann	$49,152
1970	Kathy Whitworth	$30,235
1971	Kathy Whitworth	$41,181
1972	Kathy Whitworth	$65,063
1973	Kathy Whitworth	$82,864
1974	JoAnne Carner	$87,094
1975	Sandra Palmer	$76,374
1976	Judy Rankin	$150,734
1977	Judy Rankin	$122,890
1978	Nancy Lopez	$189,814
1979	Nancy Lopez	$197,489
1980	Beth Daniel	$231,000
1981	Beth Daniel	$206,998
1982	JoAnne Carner	$310,400
1983	JoAnne Carner	$291,404
1984	Betsy King	$266,771
1985	Nancy Lopez	$416,472
1986	Pat Bradley	$492,021
1987	Ayako Okamoto	$466,034
1988	Sherri Turner	$350,851
1989	Betsy King	$654,132
1990	Beth Daniel	$863,578
1991	Pat Bradley	$763,118
1992	Dottie (Pepper) Mochrie	$693,335
1993	Betsy King	$595,992
1994	Laura Davies	$687,201
1995	Annika Sorenstam	$666,533
1996	Karrie Webb	$1,002,000
1997	Annika Sorenstam	$1,236,789
1998	Annika Sorenstam	$1,092,748
1999	Karrie Webb	$1,591,959
2000	Karrie Webb	$1,876,853
2001	Annika Sorenstam	$2,105,868
2002	Annika Sorenstam	$2,863,904
2003	Annika Sorenstam	$2,029,506
2004	Annika Sorenstam	$2,544,707
2005	Annika Sorenstam	$2,588,240

Hogan's Car Totaled in Near-Fatal Accident

On February 2, 1949, the driver's side on Ben Hogan's car was demolished after a collision with a bus on a fog-shrouded highway near Van Horn, Texas. The car's steering column was shoved through the driver's seat. Ben's life was probably saved when he threw himself to the right to shield his wife, Valerie, from the crash.

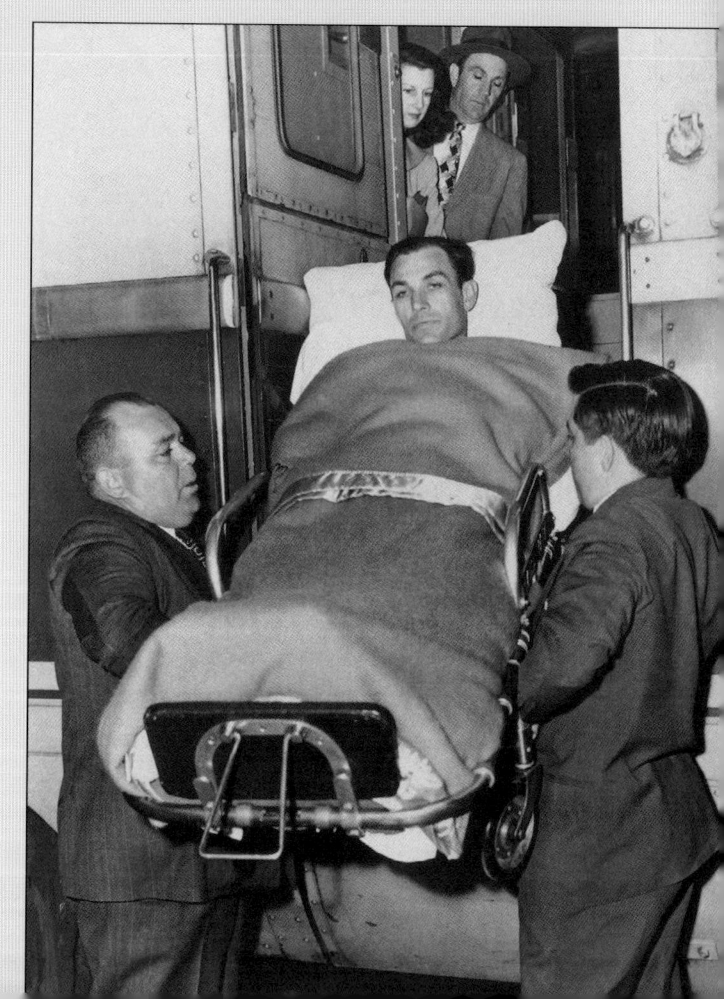

Hogan Forced to Rest His Weary Legs

A fatigued Ben Hogan *(seated, right)* was forced to rest on a shooting stick in his 1950 Los Angeles Open playoff battle with Sam Snead. Hogan's legs, severely injured in the highway crash the previous year, couldn't stand the strain of his fifth straight competitive round. Snead won the playoff, 72–76.

Hogan Wins U.S. Open in Miraculous Comeback

Doctors weren't sure whether Ben Hogan would survive the injuries from his car crash: His left leg was crushed, and his left collarbone, pelvis, and a rib were fractured. In March, he underwent emergency surgery to remove life-threatening blood clots.

The next June, just 16 months after the accident, he entered the U.S. Open at Merion, opening with rounds of 72–69, good for a tie for fifth. Each night, Hogan unwrapped the bandages that stretched from his ankles to his thighs and soaked in a tub of hot water.

Hogan was three strokes ahead in the final round, but his legs throbbed in pain, and his caddie had to pick his ball out of the hole. Hitting his tee shot at the 12th, he nearly fell. He staggered toward Harry Radix, a friend who was standing nearby. "Let me hang on to you, Harry," he gasped. "My God, I don't think I can finish."

On the second shot on the final hole, he hit one of the most famous shots in golf. With his familiar, precise swing, Hogan hit a low, boring shot that climbed to the top of a perfect arc and settled safely on the green, 40 feet from the hole. In agony, he two-putted for a tie. The following day Hogan provided a fairy-tale ending, triumphing in the playoff to win his second U.S. Open.

Incredibly, Ben Hogan was back. Just a year after an automobile accident nearly took his life, Hogan was in a playoff with Sam Snead for the 1950 Los Angeles Open title. Hogan found tree trouble here on the 5th hole and bogied, but his presence in the playoff was considered nothing short of a miracle.

"I'm only scared of **three** things: **lightning**, a **sidehill putt**, and **Ben Hogan**."

—Sam Snead

Only pretty women could separate Leo Diegel (left) and Walter Hagen (right), who were fast friends off the golf course. On the course, in serious competition, Hagen had a way of playing on the nerves of his pal. But in 1928, Diegel prevailed to win the PGA Championship and stop Hagen's four-straight winning streak in the event.

Tossin' and Turnin'

Leo Diegel was a brilliant golfer who had the misfortune of being in his prime during the era when Walter Hagen was at his peak and golf's dominant player. What's more, Diegel had a famously nervous disposition. Hagen, the master gamesman, knew of this, and while attending an all-night party on the eve of his final-round match with Diegel for the 1926 PGA Championship, Hagen was told that his opponent the next day was already in bed. Hagen replied, "Yes, but he isn't sleeping." Hagen won, 5 & 3.

Sam Snead at the 1954 Masters.

Best Masters

1942: Byron Nelson
sneaked by *Ben Hogan* by one stroke.

1954: Sam Snead
defeated *Ben Hogan* in a playoff.

1975: Jack Nicklaus
won his fifth Masters title over *Tom Weiskopf* and *Johnny Miller.*

1986: Jack Nicklaus
at 46 grabbed his sixth green jacket and 18th professional major title over *Greg Norman, Tom Kite,* and *Seve Ballesteros.*

1987: Larry Mize
upset *Greg Norman* and *Seve Ballesteros.*

2004: Phil Mickelson
took a one-stroke victory over *Ernie Els.*

"In almost all other games, you pit yourself against a mortal foe; in golf, it is yourself against the world."
—Arnold Haultain

Bobby Jones

The sum total of Bobby Jones's contributions to golf is virtually all-encompassing. He embodied the essence of golf during his competitive career. After his retirement as a player, he gave his game a golf course and a tournament that have become institutions. Augusta National and the Masters are the ultimate expressions of golf aesthetics and competitive rigor and drama.

During his eight "fat years," 1923 through 1930, this quintessential golfer became known as "Emperor Jones," and even hardened professionals who managed to beat him in an Open counted it a high achievement, if not an honor. Jones won 13 major championships from 1923 through 1930.

Jones retired from championship golf at the age of 28 and soon put in motion his dream to build a golf course. He found a perfect piece of property some 120 miles east of Atlanta in Augusta, Georgia.

Jones clearly articulated his criteria for the new course. It would give the average golfer a fair chance while requiring the utmost from top players. But most significantly, the fairways would be wide, there would be no rough, and the course would include only 29 bunkers.

Construction began in early 1932, with Jones hitting many shots from the projected tees and fairways to ascertain the proper angles, sight lines, distances, and playability of each hole. The grand opening was on January 13, 1933. The weather didn't cooperate, but golf was played, and Jones, on January 14, shot an incredible round of 69. Augusta National had been properly christened.

At the height of his game from 1923 through 1930, Jones won the U.S. Amateur five times, the U.S. Open four times, the British Open three times, and the British Amateur once.

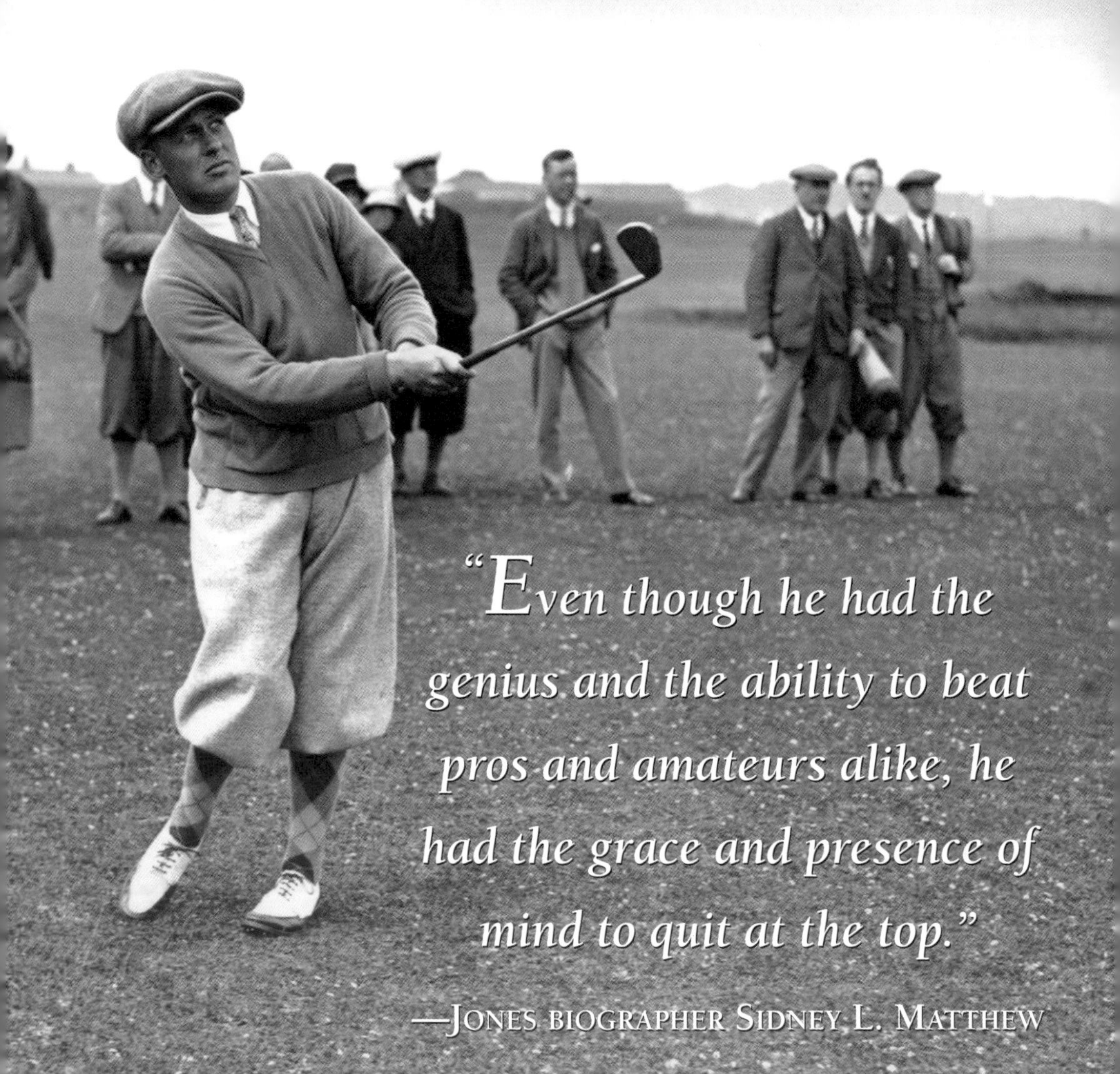

"Even though he had the genius and the ability to beat pros and amateurs alike, he had the grace and presence of mind to quit at the top."

—Jones biographer Sidney L. Matthew

Bing Crosby and Bob Hope clown it up on the greens.

CHAPTER TWO

A HOLE IN FUN:

THE LIGHTER SIDE OF GOLF

Although many take their golf extremely seriously, the game always has room for a lighter touch.

Lee Trevino

"No one who ever had lessons would have a swing like mine," Lee Trevino once said. Yet no one disputes Trevino's status as the best ball-striker since Ben Hogan, either. In the 1990s, he was asked when he last hit a ball out of bounds. He couldn't remember—nor could anyone else.

At the 1968 U.S. Open, Trevino became the first to win a U.S. Open with all four rounds in the 60s. The brilliant golf, combined with a quick wit delivered with the panache of a stand-up comic, turned him into a favorite with the gallery. "I played the tour in 1967 and told jokes and nobody laughed," he said. "Then I won the Open the next year, told the same jokes, and everybody laughed like hell."

From 1968 to 1984 on the PGA Tour, Trevino won 29 times. These wins included another U.S. Open, two PGA Championships, and two British Opens.

"One of the nice things about the Senior Tour," Trevino joked, "is that we can take a cart and a cooler. If your game is not going well, you can always have a picnic."

"He told me just to keep the ball low."

—Chi Chi Rodriguez, on the advice his caddie gave on a putt

Tom Thumb Courses Pop Up All Over

Miniature golf courses, also known as "Tom Thumbs," were a big fad in the 1920s and 1930s. In fact, by the summer of 1930, it was estimated that $125 million had been invested in Tom Thumbs in the United States. This little layout was constructed in New York City. Note the lights strung on the lines above, indicating night play.

"*Golf* and *sex* are about the only things you can enjoy without being *good* at it."

—Jimmy Demaret

Murray, Rodney Yuck It Up in *Caddyshack*

Bill Murray plea-bargains with a gopher during the 1980 film *Caddyshack*, perhaps the most popular golf movie of all time. It was certainly the funniest golf movie, with Murray, Chevy Chase, Ted Knight, and Rodney Dangerfield at their wackiest. The film's plot, though, was flimsy; it mostly poked fun at the WASPy country club set.

Walter Hagen

Walter Hagen was the first American professional golfer—he made his living only by playing the game.

Playing at the highest level from 1914 to 1936, he won 44 events, including two U.S. Opens, four British Opens, and a record-setting five PGA Championships, four of them in a row (1924 to 1927).

In some 4,000 18-hole outings from 1914 to 1941, Hagen brought in an estimated $1 million.

He was "Barnum and Bailey rolled into one."

—*Herb Graffis*

His way of walking, head tilted up like royalty, along with the lifestyle he developed, earned Hagen the sobriquet "Sir Walter."

"I don't want to be a millionaire, I just want to live like one."

—*Walter Hagen*

"The way I putted, I must have been reading the greens in *Spanish* and putting them in *English*."

—Homero Blancas

Ruth Blasts Mammoth Homers, Behemoth Drives

When he wasn't cracking home runs for the New York Yankees (he hit 60 in 1927), Babe Ruth spent considerable time on the golf course. In 1929, he reportedly drove a golf ball 325 yards using his 45-inch long "bludgeon," and in 1932 he was named president of the American Left-handers Golf Association.

No Time to Govern

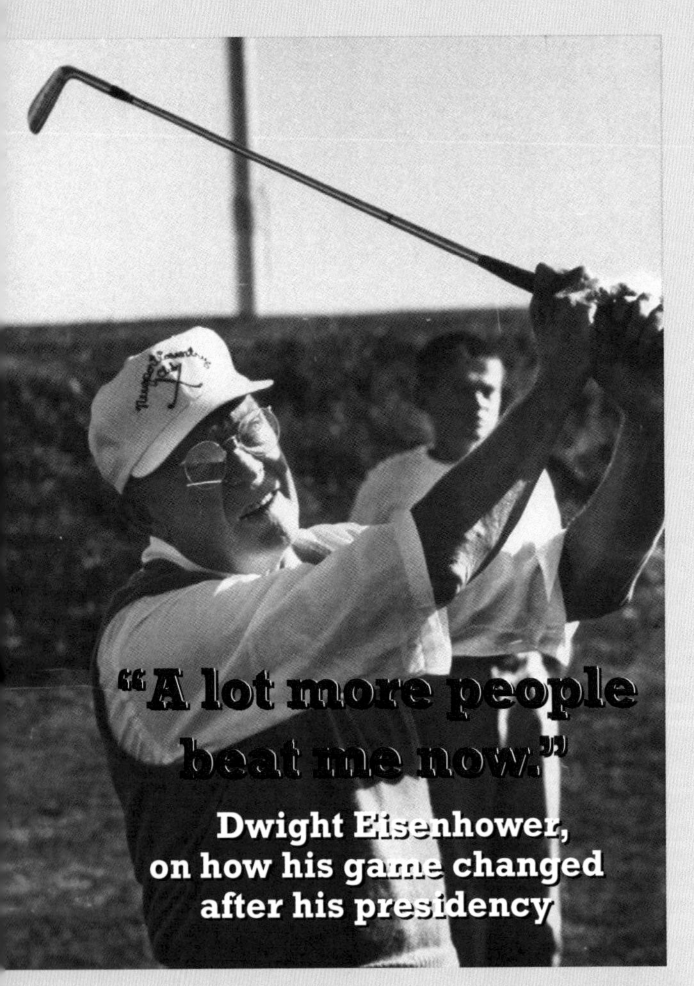

"A lot more people beat me now."

Dwight Eisenhower, on how his game changed after his presidency

According to some reports, President Dwight Eisenhower made 29 trips to Augusta National Golf Club while in office. Another calculation was that he played 800 rounds of golf during the eight years of his presidency—that would have been one round every four days, a large number even for a retiree.

A number of Americans thought Ike was on the golf course too much. A bumper sticker that popped up during his time in the White House read: "Ben Hogan for President. If we're going to have a golfer, let's have a good one."

Crosby Drops Handicap to 2

Bing Crosby *(center)* poses with Macdonald Smith *(left)* and Walter Hagen. Crosby, a caddie as a child, revived his interest in the game around 1932. In the early 1930s, he pared his handicap down to 2. In 1937, he hosted the first Bing Crosby Pro-Am, which he presided over for the remaining 40 years of his life. Among his many golf claims to fame was his 1948 hole-in-one on Cypress Point Club's 16th hole—a 233-yard hole with a green surrounded by rocks and crashing ocean waves.

Best Characters

Titanic Thompson would golf right-handed and lose, then "foolishly" bet his foes that he could beat them left-handed the next day. He'd win because he was a natural left-hander.

John "Mysterious" Montague showed up in Hollywood in the 1930s and quickly became a hit with such celebrities as Bing Crosby and Oliver Hardy. He once beat Crosby in a one-hole match using a baseball bat, a shovel, and a rake.

Lefty Stackhouse was known for his temper. After a bad shot, he might punch himself in the face, kick himself in the shin, or butt his head against a tree.

Babe Zaharias wisecracked with the galleries as she played, and sometimes after a round she would pull out her harmonica and entertain.

Jimmy Demaret was an accomplished player who won three Masters and 31 events on the PGA Tour, but he might have won more if he'd spent more time practicing and less time being the life of the party. On the course, he was the first pro to sport a highly colorful wardrobe.

One of the finest players of the 1950s was **Tommy Bolt**, but he was just as famous for his club-throwing temper tantrums and his run-ins with officials as he was for winning 15 tournaments.

During the 1960s and early '70s, **Doug Sanders** was the Tour's prince of pastels. He'd often wear one color from head to foot, favoring tones such as canary yellow, shocking pink, or robin's egg blue.

◀ **Chi Chi Rodriguez** delighted spectators with his huge swing and gregarious personality. He constantly chatted and quipped with fans and celebrated putts by tossing his hat over the hole and engaging in a mock sword dance.

Gary McCord never won a tournament, though he would occasionally liven up a pressroom after a rare appearance on the leaderboard and talk about being an alien from the planet Blothar. That brand of humor led to a far more successful career as a CBS announcer.

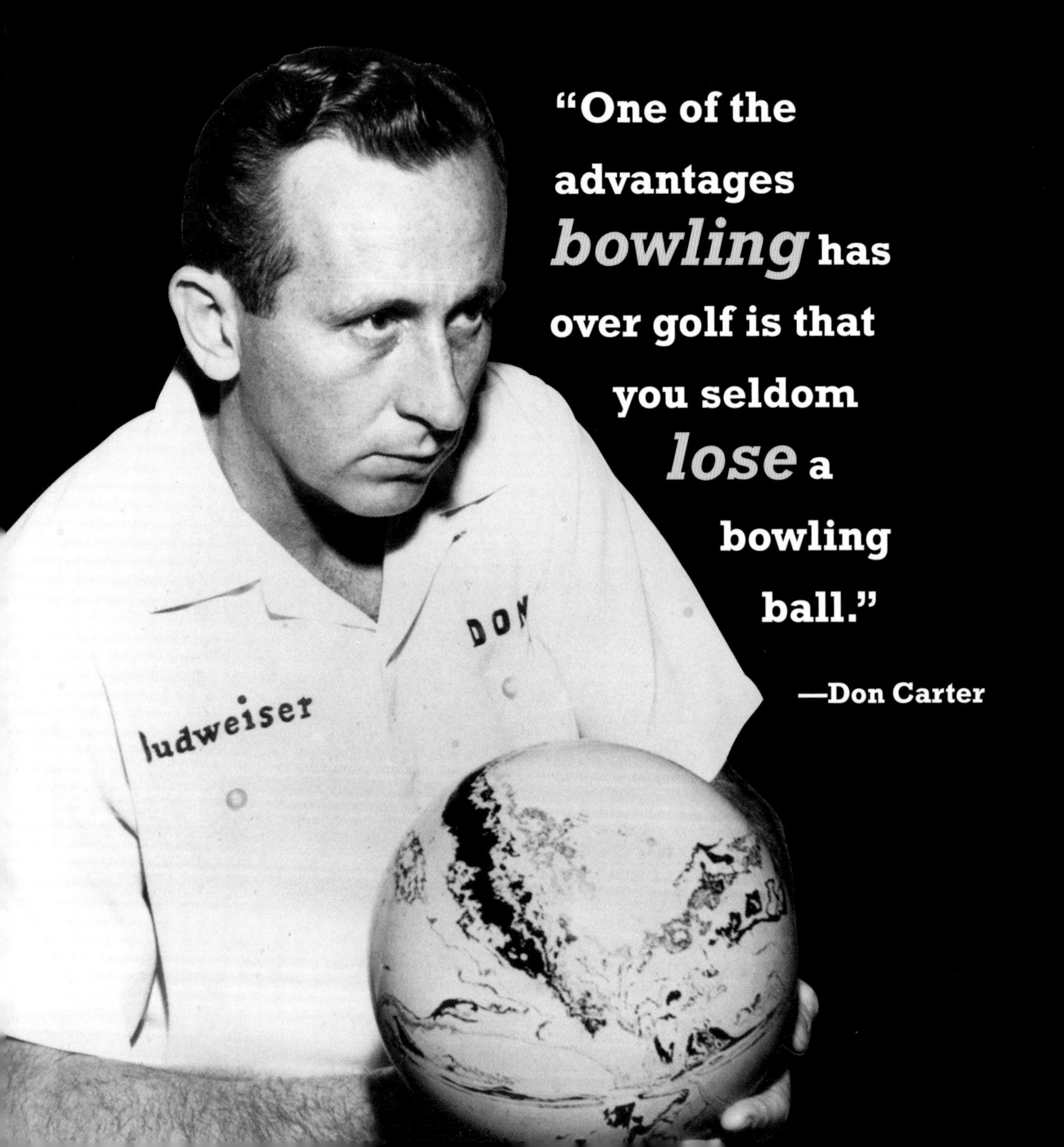
"One of the
advantages
bowling has
over golf is that
you seldom
lose a
bowling
ball."
—Don Carter
DON

Pate Takes a Swim After Winning in Memphis

Jerry Pate dives into a lake near the 18th green at Colonial Country Club, the site of his victory in the 1981 Danny Thomas Memphis Classic. Pate had earlier said if he won the tournament, he would "bathe in victory," and he made good on his promise.

"My CAREER started off slowly and then TAPERED off."

—Gary McCord

Golf Inventions Border on the Ridiculous

Some poor chaps probably shelled out good money for this silly contraption from about 1925, which would supposedly improve their golf swing. Throughout the 20th century, the U.S. Patent Office was flooded with inventions guaranteed to make golfers play like Walter Hagen, Ben Hogan, or Jack Nicklaus. Few of the greats ever used such gadgetry.

Wilson
SPORTING GOODS CO.

Babe Didrikson Zaharias

Mildred "Babe" Didrikson was an All-America basketball player in high school, a proficient swimmer and diver, an expert rifle shot, a boxer, a speedball softball pitcher, a top-notch bowler, and a tennis player of championship caliber. In the 1932 Olympic Games in Los Angeles, she won two golds and a silver, setting world records in the javelin and the 80-meter hurdles.

Cashing in on her fame, Didrikson toured in vaudeville, dancing and playing the harmonica. More interested in sports, she left show business and played professional basketball and some exhibition baseball, throwing an inning's worth of pitches for the Philadelphia Phillies in a game against the Brooklyn Dodgers.

She had been nicknamed "Babe" as a teenager after hitting five home runs in a baseball game. After marrying professional wrestler George Zaharias in 1938, she added his last name to hers.

Her competitive golf career began in earnest during World War II (1942–45). In 1945, she won her third Western Open, and in 1946 and 1947, won 14 amateur tournaments in a row, including the 1946 U.S. Women's Amateur and the 1947 British Women's Amateur.

Turning pro, Zaharias help to re-form the Women's Professional Golf Association into the Ladies PGA and became one of its major attractions—her showbiz instincts were never far from the surface. From 1948 through 1955, she won 31 professional tournaments, including three U.S. Women's Opens.

The only thing Zaharias couldn't beat was cancer. She died in September 1956 at 45.

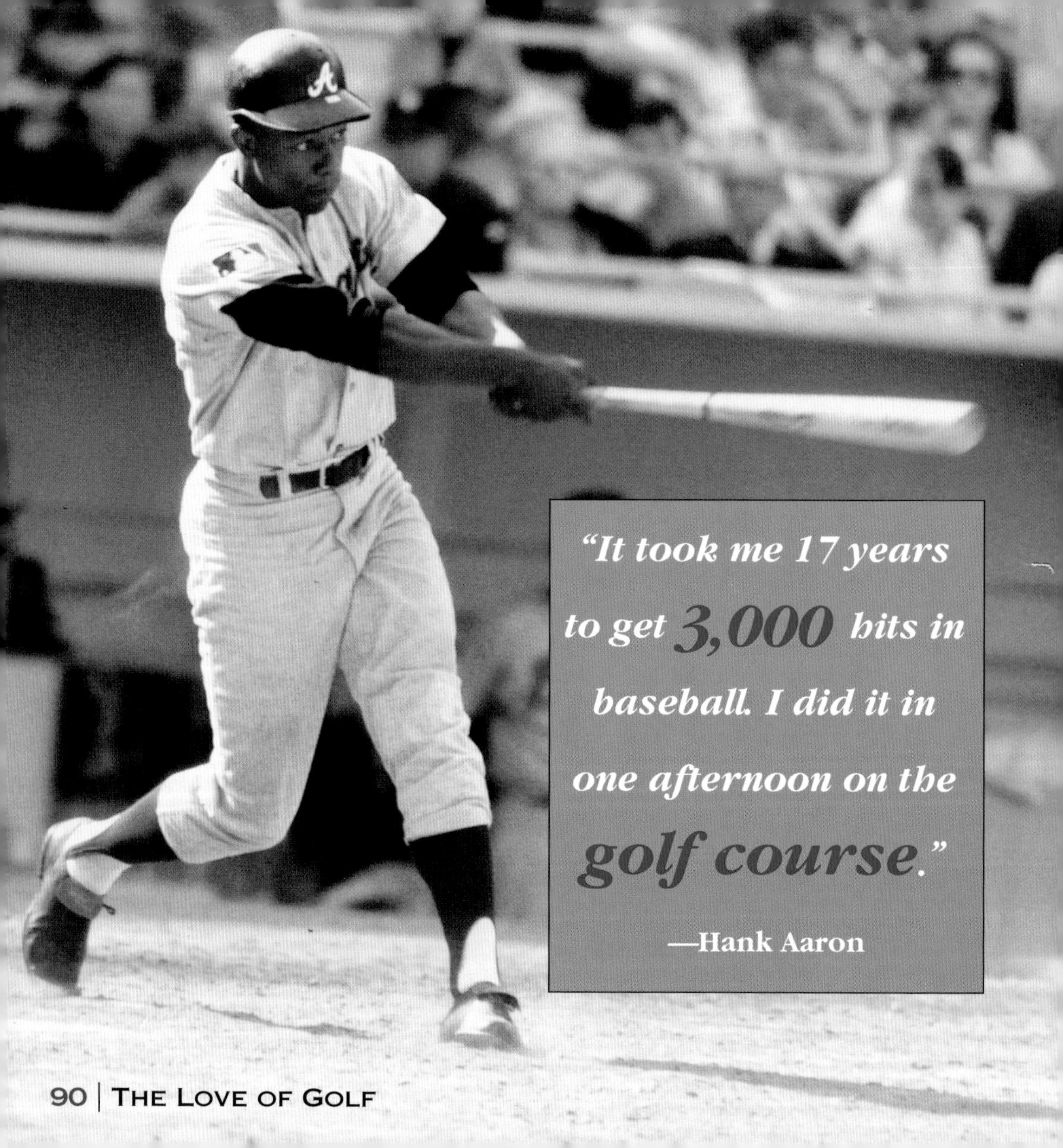

"It took me 17 years to get 3,000 hits in baseball. I did it in one afternoon on the golf course."

—Hank Aaron

USGA's New Tree Blocks Hinkle's Shortcut

Pictured is the most famous tree in golf history. The 1979 U.S. Open was held at the Inverness Club in Toledo, Ohio, and during the first round Lon Hinkle took a shortcut. He cut the dogleg on the par-5 8th hole by hitting onto the 17th fairway. Overnight, USGA officials planted this tree to block the shortcut.

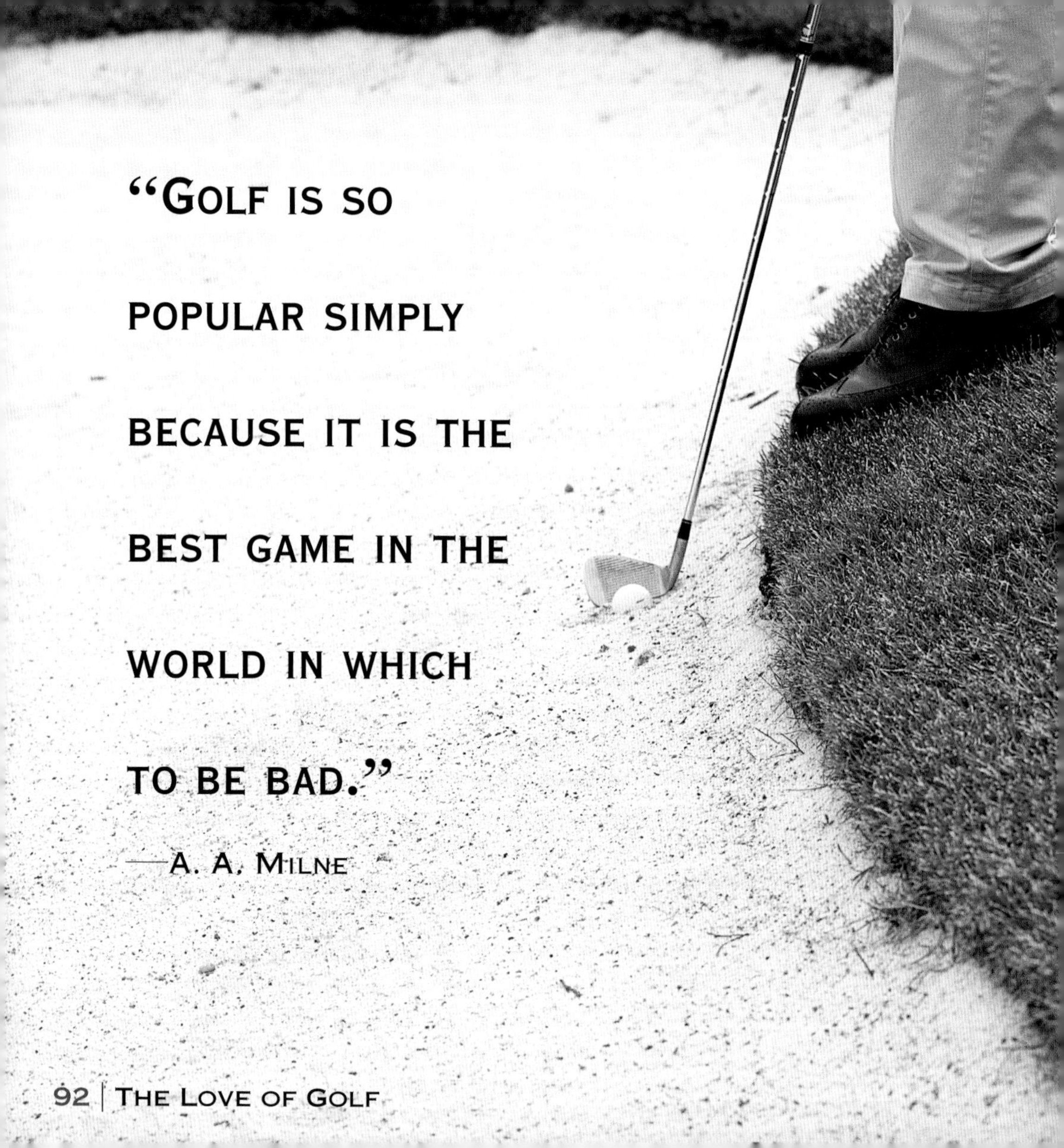

"Golf is so popular simply because it is the best game in the world in which to be bad."

—A. A. Milne

Fields Loves Golf but Is No Fan of Geese

In the 1910s, W. C. Fields kept fans in stitches with his comic golf routine. Fields loved golf and once bought a house adjacent to a golf course—although the geese that flocked around a water hazard often got on his nerves. One morning, Fields stormed out of his house in a bathrobe, waving a niblick. "Either poop green or get off my lawn!" he screamed.

Longest Drivers

The longest hitter ever is probably ▼ **Jason Zuback**, who won the National (now World) Long Drive Championship four straight times from 1996 to 1999.

Jimmy Thomson routinely boomed the ball 300 yards.

George Bayer once drove the ball past the pin on a 445-yard hole.

Jack Nicklaus supplanted Bayer as the game's longest hitter—he simply overpowered courses.

Jim Dent sometimes achieved length at the expense of accuracy.

John Jacobs won about one hundred long-drive contests around the world.

Evan "Big Cat" Williams was the first celebrity to emerge from the National Long Drive Championship.

John Daly led the PGA Tour in driving distance every year but one from 1991 through 2002.

Tiger Woods hits the ball nearly as long as Daly.

Hank Kuehne led the 2003 PGA Tour with an average of 321.4 yards.

"THE HARDEST SHOT IS A MASHIE AT 90 YARDS FROM THE GREEN, WHERE THE BALL HAS TO BE PLAYED AGAINST AN OAK TREE, BOUNCED BACK INTO A SAND TRAP, HITS A STONE, BOUNCES ON THE GREEN, AND THEN ROLLS INTO THE CUP. THAT SHOT IS SO DIFFICULT, I HAVE ONLY MADE IT ONCE."

—ZEPPO MARX

Zeppo, Groucho, Chico, and Harpo Marx

Golf at Sea

The popularity of golf knew no bounds in the 1930s—people wanted to play the game wherever they went. This miniature golf course, which featured artificial grass, was on the the sun deck of the SS *Ile de France*, the flagship of the French Line.

"IF PROFANITY HAD ANY INFLUENCE ON THE FLIGHT OF THE BALL, THE GAME WOULD BE PLAYED FAR BETTER THAN IT IS."

—HORACE HUTCHINSON

Terrible Tommy Throws a Fit in Tucson

Tommy Bolt earned the reputation of "Terrible Tommy" for his temper tantrums on the course. Here we see the Terrible One toss his putter after missing a short putt in the 1953 Tucson Open. Nevertheless, Bolt came back and shot a final-round 65 to win by one stroke over Chandler Harper.

Jimmy Demaret

Demaret triumphed in three Masters and 28 other tournaments on the PGA Tour.

With an infectious smile and jolly laugh, he told jokes with a relish.

Asked if he would have won more had he taken golf more seriously, Demaret answered, "If I had, I wouldn't have won anything."

After seeing bolts of lightweight materials in a kaleidoscope of bright colors, he ordered some golf shirts and slacks—it made no difference to him that the material was intended for ladies' garments.

"I know I got drunk last night, but how did I wind up in Squaw Valley?"

—Jimmy Demaret, on waking up to see Pebble Beach covered with snow

“I can airmail the golf ball, but sometimes I don’t put the right address on it.”

—Jim Dent

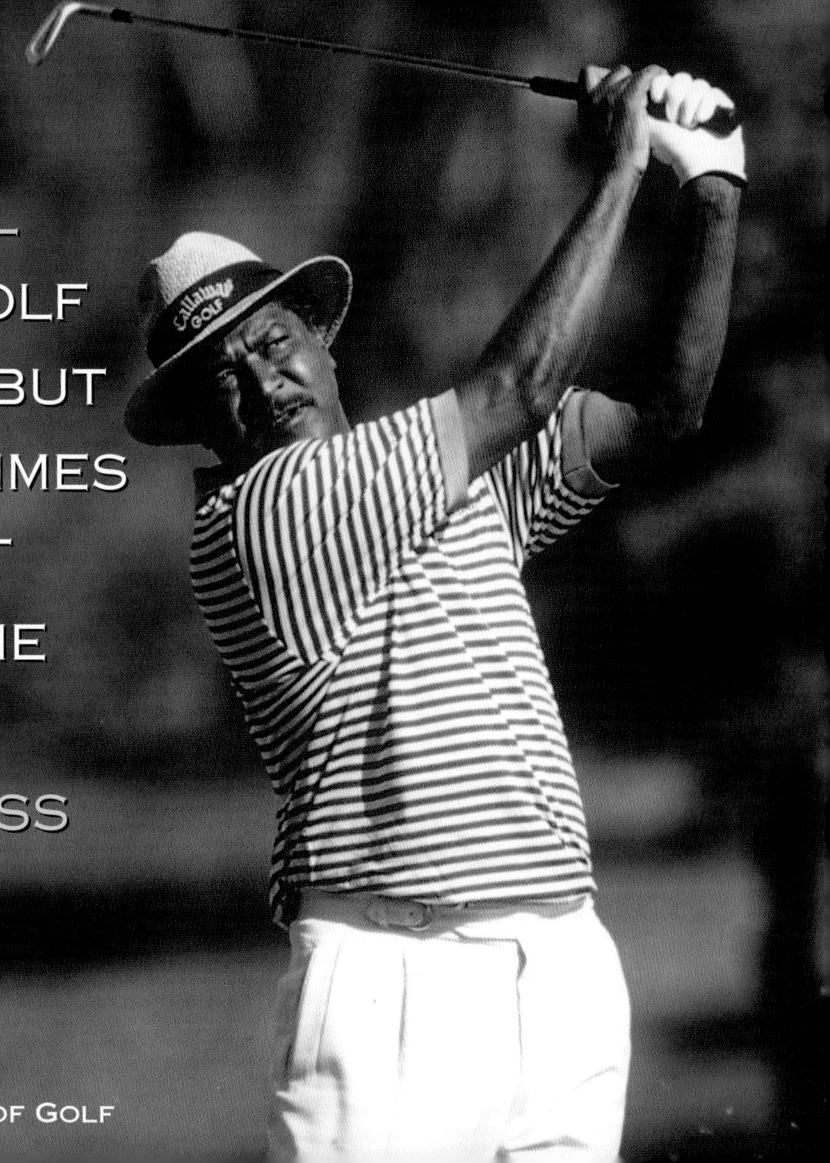

Thomson Puts on a Show with Big Drives

Jimmy Thomson's capacity to hit long drives made the long-drive contest an integral part of the PGA Tour's "pregame show." Thomson won a contest in 1937 by averaging 340 yards. Here, he pounds out a long drive at the 1936 PGA Championship at Pinehurst.

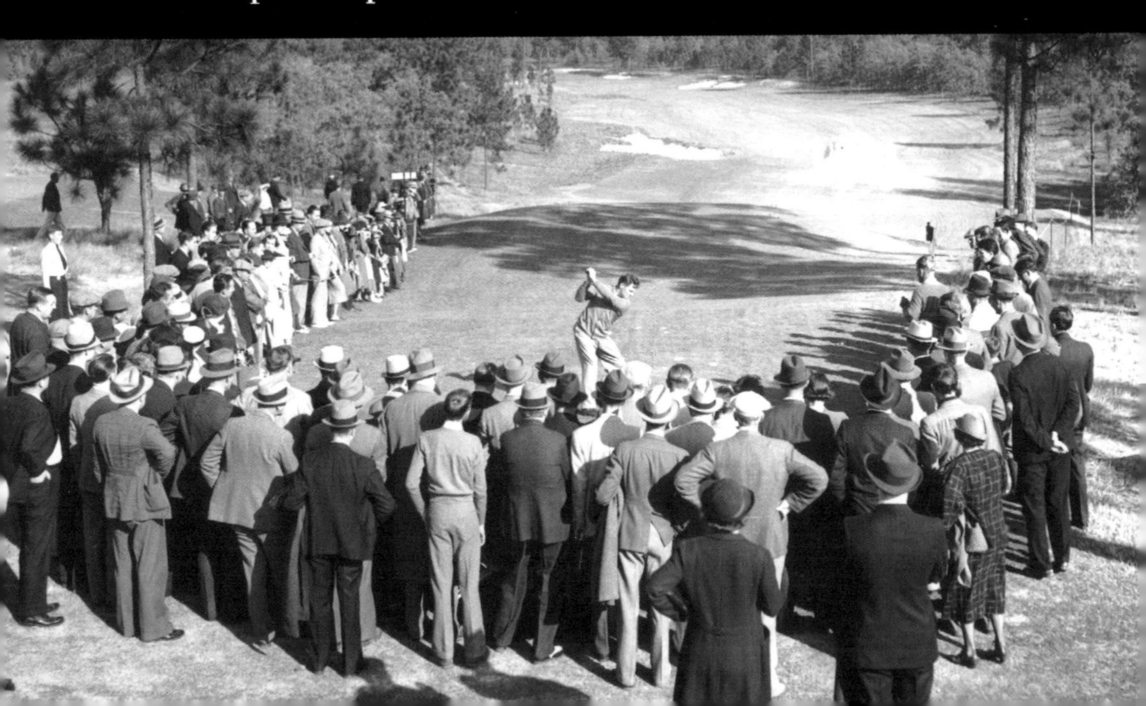

"*Never* bet with anyone you meet on the 1st tee who has a deep suntan, a 1-iron in his bag, and squinty eyes."

—Dave Marr, 1965 PGA Player of the Year

Kirkwood Reaches Into His Bag of Tricks

In 1938, Joe Kirkwood completed yet another of his world tours giving trick-shot exhibitions. By now, he had accumulated an incredible array of clubs with which he performed feats that amazed his audiences. Kirkwood was the first golfer to make his living by doing trick shots, and a good living it was.

Nicklaus Downs Sanders—Literally—in British Playoff

Not only did Jack Nicklaus beat Doug Sanders in a playoff in the 1970 British Open, but Nicklaus almost conked Sanders on the head with his putter. After sinking the winning shot at St. Andrews, Jack threw the club sky-high, not noticing his opponent's whereabouts. Nicklaus won the playoff, 72–73, after they had tied at 283.

Maltbie Wins Two in a Row, Loses Check

Roger Maltbie captured back-to-back tournaments as a Tour rookie in 1975—the Quad Cities Open in Illinois and the Pleasant Valley Classic in Massachusetts. He also made a rookie mistake at the latter event, as he accidentally left his $40,000 winner's check in a restaurant near the course. The sponsor issued him a new check.

Strangest Moments

A mobster named Machine Gun Jack McGurn, an alleged hit man with Al Capone's gang, was a wanted man in 1933. He entered the Western Open in Chicago under his real name, Vince Gebhardi. A judge issued a warrant for his arrest, and in the second round a detective read him the warrant on the 7th fairway.

Ray Ainsley's name would be forgotten if not for one notable record: He posted the highest score on a hole in PGA Tour history with a 19 on the 16th at Cherry Hills in the 1938 U.S. Open.

In 1941, the USGA gave special exemptions for the U.S. Open to two Argentineans who arrived too late for qualifying. Walter Ratto barely connected with his first tee shot, which rebounded off a tree just in front of the tee and ended up behind him, leading his playing partner to say, "Am I up, or are you away?"

On the 5th hole of the second round of the 1949 British Open, Harry Bradshaw's errant tee shot rolled into the bottom half of a broken beer bottle. He could have taken a free drop, but, not knowing the rule, he swung and advanced the ball 25 yards.

Some members of Baltusrol Golf Club complained that architect Robert Trent Jones had made the par-3 4th hole too difficult when he redesigned the course for the 1954 U.S. Open. Jones asked for a club and ball and teed up on the 4th hole. He knocked it over the water fronting the green and right into the cup for an ace.

▲ **Roberto De Vicenzo** finished the fourth round of the 1968 Masters in a tie with Bob Goalby, setting up a playoff the next day—or so everybody thought. Playing partner **Tommy Aaron** had marked a 4 instead of a 3 on the 17th hole on De Vicenzo's scorecard. When De Vicenzo, without checking carefully, signed the card that way, he was obligated to take the higher score.

Larry Ziegler was happy about winning the 1969 Michigan Classic, a first-time event on the PGA Tour, until he discovered that the sponsors didn't have enough money to pay the purse. The Tour eventually picked up the tab.

"I'm hitting the *woods* great, but I'm having trouble getting *out* of them."

—Harry Toscano, pro golfer

Williams Booms 'Em in Long Drive Contest

Evan "Big Cat" Williams unleashed a tee shot of 353 yards to win the 1977 Long Drive Championship in Pebble Beach, California. "I just relax, delay the release of my hands, use strong leg action, and let 'er rip," said Williams. In the 1990s, John Daly became famous for a similar philosophy. "Grip it and rip it," Daly said.

Jack's Little Pit Stop

In the third round of the 1978 U.S. Open, Jack Nicklaus hit a perfect tee shot on the par-4 13th hole, leaving him only 30 yards from the green. But as he walked toward his ball, there came an urgent call of nature, and Nicklaus hurried to a nearby portable toilet and then returned to his business—but not very well. He mishit his second shot into a creek, played his fourth into a bunker, and took three more before holing out for a disastrous 7.

Nicklaus was queried about what happened. He explained that he had to make a pit stop. In retrospect, did it cost him the championship? "No," Nicklaus replied, "I had to go."

Hagen Lets the Good Times Roll

Walter Hagen (*seated, left*) often made a remark that epitomized his lifestyle. "Be sure to smell the flowers along the way," he said. Hagen, who journeyed all over the world giving exhibitions, traveled in a wide range of vehicles: fast trains, airplanes, Rolls-Royce automobiles, and even the occasional rickshaw, as shown here.

Chapter Three

Strokes of Genius:

Golf's Turning Points and Milestones

In one dramatic moment, our understandings and expectations of golf can change forever.

Arnold Palmer leads Arnie's Army.

Arnold Palmer

It is the rare athlete who transcends his sport to become a national folk hero. Such was the case with Arnold Palmer. Millions who watched him win the 1960 U.S. Open saw a refreshingly animated athlete filled with a visor-tossing exhilaration.

Palmer's play had an endearing quality with which the average golfer could identify. He swung hard and fast and had a less-than-classic, gyrating follow-through. He hit the ball with great authority and for distance. He took chances, "went for broke," and the crowd loved him for it. They created what came to be called "Arnie's Army," loyal followers who chased after and cheered him.

Palmer says a few words after his 1960 U.S. Open victory. Arnie shot a final-round 65 at Cherry Hills outside of Denver to overcome a seven-stroke deficit. He had already claimed the Masters earlier in the year.

Palmer's most productive stretch came from 1960 to 1963, when he won 29 Tour events. At the time, a young Jack Nicklaus was also emerging as a force in the game, and Palmer already had a heady rival in South Africa's Gary Player. The trio became known as the "Big Three," and between them they captured every Masters from 1960 to 1966.

Tied with Nicklaus for the most consecutive years winning at least one tournament (17), Palmer was the first golfer to reach $1 million in career prize money. His love for the game was also unmatched. That, along with his ready smile, an unpretentious manner that projected easy access by the gallery (he was known for never passing up an autograph request), and a readiness to talk with the press, made Arnold Palmer a household name.

Palmer's bold style endeared him to galleries, and the game enjoyed a huge boost in popularity after he emerged.

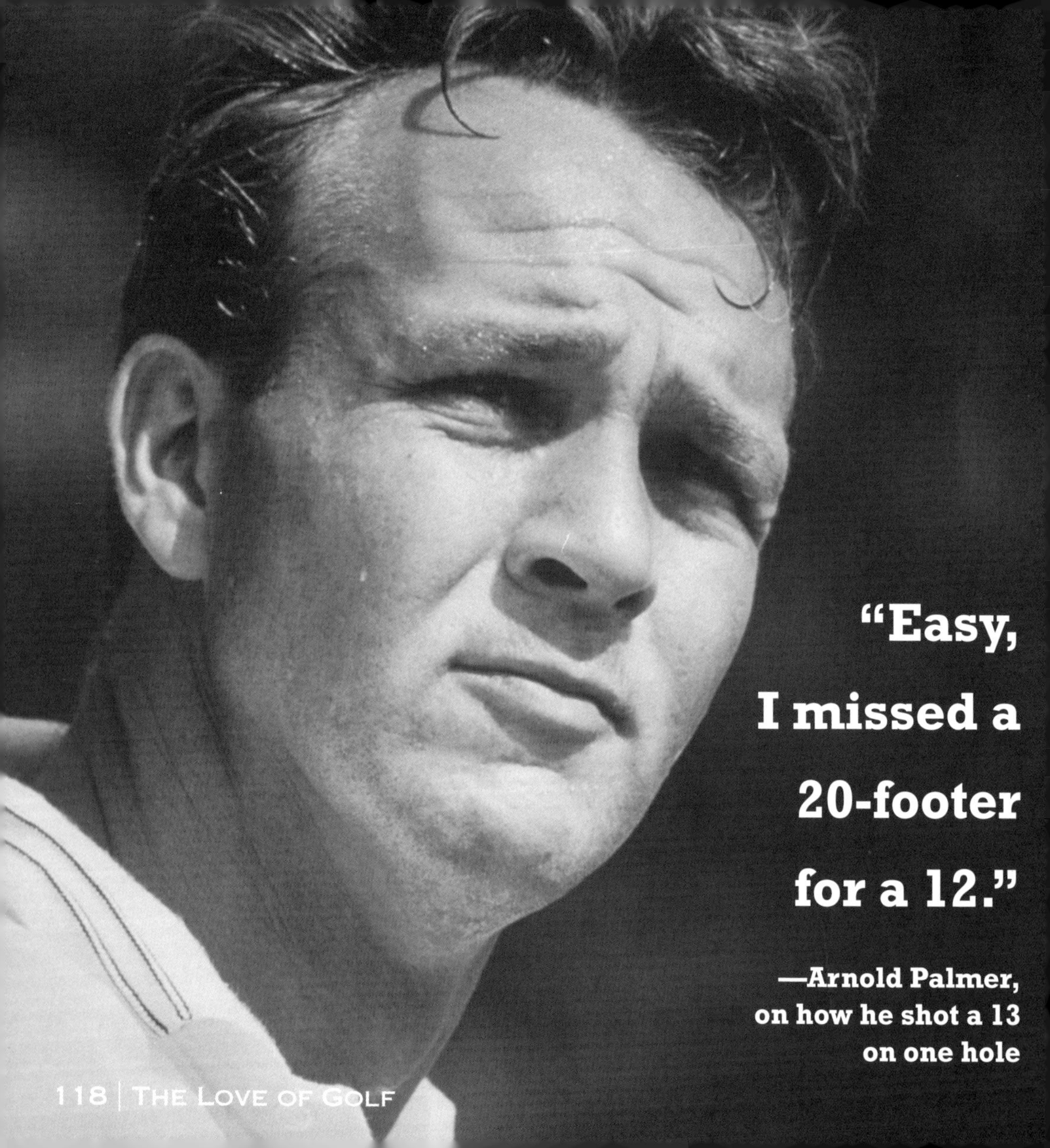

"Easy,
I missed a
20-footer
for a 12."

—Arnold Palmer,
on how he shot a 13
on one hole

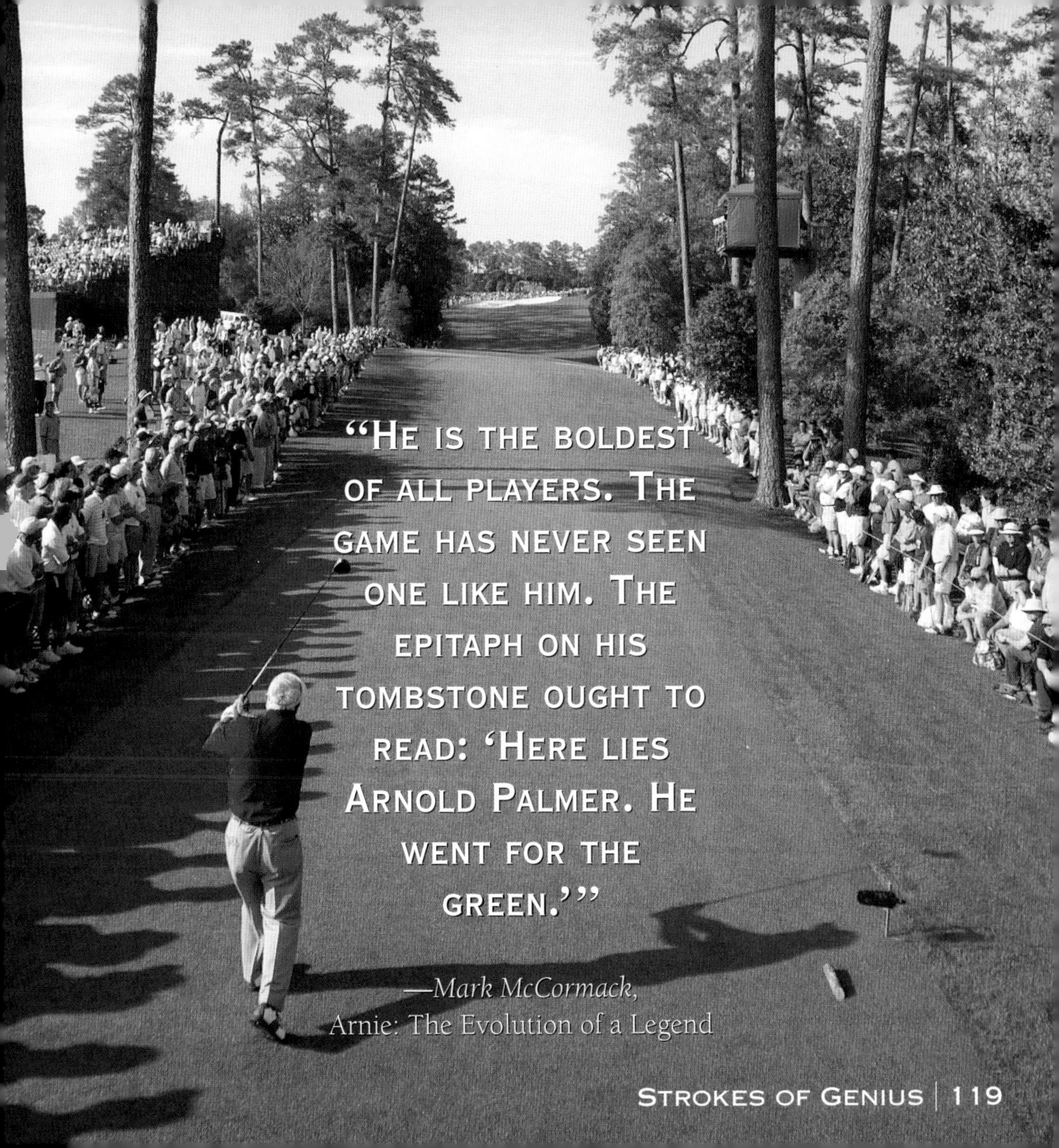

"He is the boldest of all players. The game has never seen one like him. The epitaph on his tombstone ought to read: 'Here lies Arnold Palmer. He went for the green.'"

—*Mark McCormack*,
Arnie: The Evolution of a Legend

"It is nothing new or original to say that golf is played one stroke at a time. But it took me many years to realize it."

—Bobby Jones

Jones, 15, Prevails in Southern Amateur

In 1917, Bobby Jones was a tanned teenager with skinny arms, but oh, what a golf swing. . . . The 15-year-old was good enough to capture that year's Southern Amateur in Birmingham, Alabama. Jones had first played golf on a dirt roadway at the age of six. At age nine, he won a junior tournament sponsored by the Atlanta Athletic Club.

Tiger Woods

Tiger Woods burst upon the scene in late 1996 and unquestionably became the No. 1-ranked golfer in the world. "We haven't seen anybody that good in a long time," said two-time Masters champion and noted golf historian Ben Crenshaw.

When Woods won the 2000 British Open at St. Andrews, he became just the fifth player in history to complete a career Grand Slam—victories in all four major championships: Masters, U.S. Open, British Open, and PGA Championship. A month later, he captured another PGA Championship. Woods had his fifth major title and third in a row—a feat not accomplished since Ben Hogan won the Masters, U.S. Open, and British Open in 1953. Woods won his fourth straight major, the Masters, in 2001.

His 2000 season was one for the ages: nine Tour victories, the most since Sam Snead won 11 times in 1950; three major championships; 17 top-five finishes in 20 starts; and a record scoring average of 68.17.

Eldrick "Tiger" Woods grew up in Cypress, California, under the watchful eye of father Earl. At age two, Master Woods appeared on *CBS News* and *The Mike Douglas Show*, where he putted with Bob Hope. Tiger won the U.S. Junior Amateur title for the first time at 15, then defended it the next two years. Tiger won his first U.S. Amateur at 18, becoming the youngest player to win that trophy. When he won it in 1996 for the third straight year, he did something not even Bobby Jones or Jack Nicklaus had accomplished.

When he turned pro, Woods was almost immediately in contention. He finished in the top five in five straight tournaments, something that had not been done since 1982. Then he won the Masters and four more tournaments on the Tour in 1997. All the excitement over a new champion also brought a mass audience back to golf.

Fans flock to witness Tiger in action. Even fellow pros have been amazed. As Bobby Jones once said about the "Golden Bear" himself, "He's playing a game with which I'm not familiar," said Jack Nicklaus about Woods. "He hits the ball nine million miles and without a swing that looks like he's trying to." Woods made history in 1997 when he topped Nicklaus's Masters record and set another for largest Masters margin of victory — 12 strokes.

Charles Becomes First Lefty to Win a Major

Bob Charles hoists the hardware after winning the 36-hole playoff of the 1963 British Open. Charles defeated Phil Rodgers by a full eight strokes, 140–148. In doing so, he made history: The New Zealander became the first left-handed golfer ever to win a major professional championship.

Southpaw Mickelson Explodes onto Scene

In 1990, **Phil Mickelson's** smooth swing gave hope to all left-handed golfers. Mickelson won both the NCAA championship and the U.S. Amateur, prompting comparisons to Jack Nicklaus, then the only other person to win both in the same year. (Tiger Woods has accomplished this since.) Fittingly, Phil won the 1990 Jack Nicklaus Award as collegiate player of the year.

Augusta National

It's rare when a course's fame outstrips the tournament held there, but that's the case at Augusta National. Of the four major tournaments—the Masters, the U.S. Open, the British Open, and the PGA Championship—only the Masters returns to the same site every year. Augusta National *is* the Masters.

The course, designed by Bobby Jones and architect Alister Mackenzie, opened in 1932. Each hole is adorned with a plant for which it is named. Hole 1 is Tea Olive, hole 2 is Pink Dogwood, hole 3 is Flowering Peach, and so on. Seen here is hole 13, Azalea.

The holes at Augusta National look fairly simple and can be played by the average golfer. But as architect Geoffrey Cornish and *Golf Digest*'s Ronald Whitten wrote in their book *The Golf Course:* "Every hole had a preferred target, a spot from which it was most advantageous to play the next stroke."

Augusta National may be best known for the most notorious three-hole stretch in golf—Amen Corner. *Sports Illustrated* writer Herbert Warren Wind is credited with coining the name for the section that includes the second half of the 11th, all of the 12th, and the first half of the 13th. Jack Nicklaus once noted that one of his most embarrassing moments occurred on 12: "Bobby Jones and Clifford Roberts had come down to the 12th to watch me—and I shanked the tee shot right over their heads!"

Sarazen's Sand Blaster

Gene Sarazen in 1932 conceived the idea of the first legal sand wedge. He angled a flange on the back of a niblick so the rear portion of the club hit the sand before the leading edge. One could now hit behind the ball without fear of digging too deeply.

Sarazen realized he had something special. "It got so I would bet even money I could go down in two out of the sand," he once recalled. That year, he took his wedge with him to play in the British Open.

"After every practice round, I put the club under my coat and took it back to the hotel with me," Sarazen recounted, "because if the British had seen it before the tournament began, they would have barred it. Oh, yes. Once the tournament was underway, they couldn't do that. I went down in two from most of the bunkers." And he won the championship.

Burke Wins U.S. Open Title with Steel Shafts

Billy Burke, an American of Lithuanian heritage, won the 1931 U.S. Open, at the Inverness Club in Toledo, Ohio. The one-time iron worker in the mills of Cleveland was the first winner of the national championship to use steel-shafted clubs—and the last to use the experimental "balloon" golf ball, which weighed only 1.55 ounces.

Billy Burke, center

Francis Ouimet

There was enough wonderful coincidence in Francis Ouimet's monumental U.S. Open victory in 1913 to fill a romantic heart to the fullest. Ouimet grew up a pitch-shot distance from the Country Club in Brookline, Massachusetts, where he began his golf career as a caddie. But perhaps most significant of all, he was an amateur who beat two of the best players in golf, professionals Harry Vardon and Ted Ray, in a head-to-head contest.

In those years, amateurism was far more highly regarded. Pro golfers were considered mere mercenaries and treated not unlike second-class citizens; for instance, they were not allowed into the clubhouses of private clubs. And, of course, Ouimet was an American defeating the lords of British golf. Ouimet was the first amateur to win the U.S. Open and only the second native-born American to do so. The positive repercussions of Ouimet's victory could never be measured precisely, but there is little doubt that it led to a far wider interest in golf in the United States.

Ouimet was not a fluke. A serious student of swing technique and an early investigator of the mental side of golf, he continued to play at a high level for some 20 years. He was held in such esteem that, in 1951, he became the first American to be honored as the captain of the Royal & Ancient Golf Club of St. Andrews, Scotland. He died in 1967.

The 1913 U.S. Open was a celebration of youth. The fresh-faced Ouimet was only 20 years old when he won the championship, and his caddie, Eddie Lowery, was only 10 years old.

Best Shots

A 21-year-old **Bobby Jones** claimed his first major championship with a bold shot during the 1923 U.S. Open at Inwood on Long Island. After hitting his tee shot into the rough on the 18th hole, he took a 2-iron and carried the water from 200 yards, finishing only six feet from the hole.

Tommy Armour needed an unlikely birdie on the 457-yard finishing hole of the 1927 U.S. Open at Oakmont near Pittsburgh. The man

with the reputation as one of the game's top iron players rifled a 3-iron at the flag, and the ball finished ten feet below the hole.

Time was running out for **Gene Sarazen** at the 1935 Masters on the 15th hole, a par-5 with water in front of the green. Sarazen made up three strokes on one hole by holing a 4-wood for a double eagle.

Arnold Palmer led the 1961 British Open at Royal Birkdale, but his tee shot on the 15th hole of the final round ended up at the base of a blackberry bush. Instead of pitching out with a wedge, Palmer grabbed a 6-iron and took a mighty swing. The ball finished on the green, 15 feet from the hole.

◀ **Sally Little** was still looking for her first LPGA victory as she came to the 72nd hole of the 1976 Ladies Masters at Moss Creek tied for the lead. That quickly changed, as the South African claimed her first win in style. After hitting her second shot into a bunker, she holed out from 75 feet to beat Jan Stephenson by a single stroke.

Jack Nicklaus secured his victory at the 1972 U.S. Open at Pebble Beach by firing a 1-iron into the wind on the par-3 17th and watching the ball bounce once, hit the flagstick, and stop only two inches from the hole. He later said he made a mid-swing adjustment after feeling at the top of his backswing that he might hook the ball.

Sergio Garcia's drive on the 16th hole at the 1999 PGA Championship came to rest inches from the base of a tree. Most players would have punched out with a wedge, but the fearless 19-year-old took a full swing with a 6-iron and hit a huge fade that landed on the green.

"Given an equality of strength and skill, the victory in golf will be to him who is captain of his soul."

—Arnold Haultain,
The Mystery of Golf

Elder Breaks the Color Barrier at the Masters

In 1975, Lee Elder became the first African-American golfer invited to the Masters, earning the invitation because of his victory in the 1974 Monsanto Open. Elder would eventually be inducted into the NCAA Hall of Fame—even though he never went to college. He was so honored because of his gracious contributions to colleges and the underprivileged.

PGA Tour Demands Clubs Integrate

The 1990 PGA Championship at the all-white Shoal Creek Country Club is most remembered for a controversy that raised golf's consciousness.

Shoal Creek founder Hall Thompson was quoted as saying, "The country club is our home, and we pick and choose who we want. I think we've said that we don't discriminate in every other area except the blacks."

Most clubs that had hosted PGA Championships and U.S. Opens had no African-American members, but none had publicly stated they wouldn't admit them, and their tacit discrimination was ignored. Thompson brought the issue into the spotlight.

The most immediate reaction came from African-American groups: The Southern Christian Leadership Conference and the NAACP called for picketing and protests of the tournament. More importantly, nearly all the scheduled sponsors of the ABC tournament telecast dropped their support.

The PGA of America, the PGA Tour, and the USGA declared they would no longer hold tournaments at clubs that discriminated. Clubs would not only have to say they were willing to admit African-American (or women) members but would actually have to admit them.

Protests were averted when, less than two weeks before the event, Shoal

Creek admitted Louis Willie, a local African-American businessperson, as an honorary member.

Over the next few months, nine clubs withdrew as tournament sites, including Butler National and Cypress Point from the PGA Tour, Chicago Golf Club and Merion from USGA events, and Aronimink from the 1993 PGA Championship. But many more, including Augusta National, admitted minority and/or women members in order to comply with the guidelines.

Byron Nelson

Many records are set in sports, and almost all are invariably broken. One, however, may well stand the test of time: Byron Nelson's 11 consecutive PGA victories set in 1945.

When he turned pro, Nelson took a job as professional at a Texarkana golf club. "Very seldom did anybody come to the club before noon on any day," he said. "There was an excellent practice field, so I hit balls. I hit 'em down, then hit 'em back. So I got better and better."

The year 1945 saw The Streak. Nelson was rejected from military service during World War II owing to a blood deficiency, and it has been said that his run of victories was not against the toughest possible fields. Ben Hogan and Jimmy Demaret, in the Navy at the time, played in only two of the events. However, Sam Snead had been discharged from the Navy, and he played in all but three.

In any case, stroke-play golf is essentially played against the course. During The Streak, Nelson played 38 rounds of stroke play (we omit the first victory, a four-ball in which he had a partner, as well as the match-play formatted PGA Championship), which included two 18-hole playoff rounds against Snead to decide the Charlotte Open. Throughout The Streak, Nelson amassed just 2,581 strokes, an average of 67.92 per round. In those 38 rounds, he was 113-under-par.

There is no getting around it. Nelson's streak was an unmatchable exhibition of sustained excellence. Ironically, The Streak ended when an amateur, Freddie Haas, Jr., won the Memphis Invitational. But Nelson won again the next week, and six more times for 18 victories on the year, another record that still holds and may well hold as long as the 11 in a row.

Sportswriter Herbert Warren Wind described Nelson as "a deeply pleasant and mild man . . . the first of our golfers whose technique was so grooved and compact that everyone referred to him as a machine."

"At my **best**, I **never** came close to the golf Byron Nelson **shoots**."

—Bobby Jones

"GOLF IS THE ONLY GAME IN THE WORLD IN WHICH A PRECISE KNOWLEDGE OF THE RULES CAN EARN ONE A REPUTATION FOR BAD SPORTSMANSHIP."

—PATRICK CAMPBELL, *HOW TO BECOME A SCRATCH GOLFER*

Hagen Ekes Out Fourth Straight PGA Title

From the 1916 inaugural PGA Championship through 1927 (it was at match play until 1958), Walter Hagen won 35 matches and lost three. So the five times he won the event were no surprise. The first title came in 1921, and from 1924 to 1927, Hagen won four in a row.

The 1927 PGA was played in November at the Cedar Crest Country Club in Dallas. Hagen was the favorite, but a cakewalk was not expected. A batch of young and hungry pros were anxious to make their mark.

In his fourth match, Hagen met Al Espinosa, the Spaniard out of Chicago who would go to the PGA final in 1928. Espinosa had Hagen one down with one to play before falling to "majors fever." He three-putted the 18th from 25 feet while Hagen got down in two with a great chip from a tough lie. When Espinosa three-putted again on the first extra hole, it was over.

In the final against Joe Turnesa, runner-up to Bobby Jones in the 1926 U.S. Open and conqueror of Gene Sarazen earlier in the week, Hagen was two down after 18 holes. But Turnesa allowed Hagen back in with poor play at the 21st and 22nd holes, and the champion went on to win, 1 up. Hagen had won five of the first ten PGA Championships, and he only played in eight of them.

Mr. 59!

Geiberger's the First to Break 60

On June 10, 1977, Al Geiberger became the first player to break 60 in an official PGA Tour event. His 13-under 59 in the second round of the Danny Thomas Memphis Classic electrified the sports world. He played a stretch of seven holes in 8-under, and on the 18th hole he canned an eight-footer for birdie. He won the tournament and earned the nickname "Mr. 59."

Rankin First on LPGA Tour to Reach $100,000

Judy Rankin reached an important milestone in 1976 when she became the first LPGA player to earn $100,000 in a season. Actually, Rankin soared to $150,734, thanks to six wins including the lucrative Colgate-Dinah Shore Winners Circle. Rankin also benefited from a Tour purse that jumped from $1.74 million in 1975 to $2.53 million in '76.

The National

Born in Chicago, Charles Blair Macdonald attended the University of St. Andrews, where his love of golf originated. He was one of the great U.S. players of the late 19th century, winning the first U.S. Amateur in 1895. But he always had an eye toward building his own dream course in the States. Rejecting many sites, he finally settled on a 250-acre parcel along the shores of eastern Long Island's Peconic Bay outside Southampton. Construction started in 1907, and the course opened two years later.

Macdonald modeled several holes after notable British layouts. The 271-yard 2nd is similar to the 3rd at Royal St. George's. The 3rd takes on the characteristics of the Alps at Prestwick. The 4th is a mirror image of North Berwick's Redan. The 7th and 13th re-create portions of two St. Andrews holes.

Macdonald continued tinkering with the bunkers and greens at The National. In 1928, he wrote, "I am not confident the course is perfect and beyond criticism today." Many would disagree.

The windmill near the 16th green is one of many picturesque scenes at The National.

Seve Ballesteros

Born in Pedreña in rural northern Spain, Ballesteros turned professional at 17.

At 19, he finished in a tie for second with Jack Nicklaus in the 1976 British Open won by Johnny Miller.

Ballesteros has won more than 60 tournaments around the world, including three British Opens and two Masters.

A potent figure in the revival of interest in the Ryder Cup Matches, he played on the European team eight times from 1979 to 1995 and was captain in 1997.

Ballesteros's popularity ignited the explosive growth of the European Tour.

STEROS

“Golf is an indispensable adjunct to high civilization.”

—Andrew Carnegie

Taylor Gets It Right with Dimpled Ball

Early on, ball-makers had experimented with all sorts of wild geometries. But in Great Britain in 1905, William Taylor patented a cover with a concave dimple pattern. The dimpled ball was more aerodynamic than other versions, and similar patterns are still in use today.

The Ghost of Billy Joe Patton

In the 1954 Masters, North Carolinian Billy Joe Patton made a serious run at the title. Patton still had the lead going to the dogleg-left par-5 13th hole, where he decided to go for the green with his second shot. He mishit, and the ball went into the creek before the green, the beginning of the end for his hopes of an upset.

Ben Crenshaw

Thirty years later, Ben Crenshaw, leading the tournament by a slender margin, came to the same 13th hole. Crenshaw knew of Patton's demise. Still, he contemplated going for the green.

Crenshaw said he looked into the gallery for his father and some sign of what to do. His eye instead fell on a beam of sunlight filtering through the pines that spotlighted Billy Joe Patton. This was a vision, for Patton, an official at the tournament, wasn't anywhere near the scene. Crenshaw opted not to go for it. He laid up short of the creek, then went on to win his first major title.

Smith Wins by One in First Masters

Horton Smith won the first Masters Tournament (known then as Augusta National Invitational) in 1934 with rounds of 70–72–70–72—284. Smith canned a 20-foot birdie putt on the 17th to take a one-stroke lead over Craig Wood, who had finished. Horton maintained his lead with a par on the final hole. Smith would capture the Masters title again in 1936.

Nicklaus Edges Popular Palmer in U.S. Open

The 1962 U.S. Open was the setting for one of those classic encounters that marks the end of one era and the beginning of another. Arnold Palmer, the darling of the galleries, was outdueled by Jack Nicklaus, a stocky rookie with a stoic playing style. Their playoff marked the end of Palmer's reign as golf's undisputed king.

The U.S. Open was held at Oakmont Country Club, near Palmer's hometown of Latrobe, Pennsylvania. In addition to the usual members of Arnie's Army, his gallery was swelled by local admirers. "They were out in full force—and full throat," said Nicklaus, who was paired with Palmer the first two rounds.

After dominating the amateur ranks, Nicklaus was in his first season as a pro. Immensely talented, he hit the ball prodigious distances and enjoyed a delicate putting touch on the greens.

With ten holes to go, Arnie had a three-stroke lead, and it was his U.S. Open to win. The 480-yard, par-5 9th hole was pivotal. Nicklaus birdied. Behind him, Palmer fluffed a greenside chip, bogied, and saw his lead shrink to one. When Palmer hit a bunker and bogied the short 13th, they were tied. Both men finished at 283.

The playoff gallery belonged to Palmer. As noisy as wrestling fans, a few shouted insults at Nicklaus. Unfazed, the stoic, deliberate Nicklaus shot a 71. Palmer lost with a 74. Nicklaus cut short the Palmer era and began an era of his own.

Newcomer Webb Gathers $1 Million

Rookie Karrie Webb became the first million-dollar woman on the LPGA Tour when she was victorious at the 1996 season-ending ITT LPGA Tour Championship. Her fourth win of the year gave her an LPGA-record $1,002,000 for the season. The Australian opened the campaign by finishing second and first in her first two events, and she barely slowed down all year.

"Nothing contributes *more* to the popularity of golf than the almost *endless* variety."

—John L. Low,
19th-century golfer and author

Britain's Great Triumvirate Rules Supreme

In ancient Rome, the job of leadership was, for a time, shared by three men—a "triumvirate," from the Latin. Leadership of the world of golf at the turn of the 20th century was also the property of a triumvirate: Britons Harry Vardon, John Henry Taylor, and James Braid.

How dominant was the Great Triumvirate? One merely has to examine the record. In the 21 years from 1894 to 1914, the three compiled 16 first-place finishes and a dozen seconds in the British Open. In golf-mad Britain, Vardon, Braid, and Taylor were heroes.

Wherever they played, the Triumvirate was followed by adoring, tumultuous galleries. Newspapers often published praise for their prowess, photographs, and endless descriptions of matches, strokes, and victories. But none phrased it better than Horace Hutchinson, the great English amateur and author, when he wrote: "The three great men . . . had this in common, that they all took the game earnestly and kept themselves very fit and well, in order to do their best in it; therein marking a point of departure from the usual mode of the Scottish professional of the old days, who was a happy-go-lucky fellow, not taking all the care of himself that he should if he was to excel in such a strenuous game as golf. The example of these men was infectious."

Indeed it was. One wonders if it hadn't been for the Triumvirate, would golf have ever attained the station in society it now occupies? Or would we all be playing croquet, lawn bowling, and/or cricket?

John Henry Taylor, James Braid, Harry Vardon

A Kid Named Palmer Wins U.S. Amateur

Arnold Palmer, age 24, began his reign as golf's most charismatic player by winning the 1954 U.S. Amateur. Palmer edged Robert Sweeny, 1 up, in a thrilling final at the Country Club of Detroit.

Woods Wins, Turns Pro, and Keeps On Winning

Tiger Woods added to his legend by winning an unprecedented third straight U.S. Amateur in 1996, with a stirring comeback keyed by a 30-foot birdie putt on the next-to-last hole of regulation against Steve Scott. Woods then turned pro, signed a big contract with Nike, and won two tournaments in his first eight PGA Tour starts.

Berg Prevails in the First Women's Open

Patty Berg, a savvy player with an efficient swing, won the first U.S. Women's Open in 1946. Her career included a record 15 major wins. Berg battled with Louise Suggs for supremacy in the 1950s, and both wound up in the LPGA Hall of Fame.

"In the early days, there was not much of a future for women pros in golf after tournament life. There were very few if any club jobs available. But I don't know that any of us were prepared for living without tournament golf."

—Betsy Rawls

"Long driving, if it be not the most deadly, is certainly the most dashing and fascinating part of the game; and of all others the principal difficulty of the golfer to acquire."

—H. B. Farnie,
author of 1857's *The Golfer's Manual*,
golf's first instructional book

The 647-Yard Double-Eagle

Neither wind nor rain—nor typhoons—seem to be able to stop the appointed rounds of a golfer. Playing at the Guam Navy Golf Club on January 3, 1982, after a typhoon had just passed, Chief Petty Officer Kevin Murray had a 40-mph wind to deal with, and it certainly helped him on the 647-yard par-5. Hitting on a hard fairway with the wind at his back, his drive was later measured at 387 yards. Then Murray took a 4-iron, which hit about 20 yards short of the green, bounced, and rolled into the cup for the longest double-eagle ever recorded.

Legends of Golf Sows Seeds for Senior Tour

Fred Raphael, TV producer of *Shell's Wonderful World of Golf*, had a new project. Called The Legends of Golf, it would bring together greats of the game's past, 50 years and older, for a competition.

Raphael found a buyer in NBC, and in 1978 the Legends was born. The first Legends, won by Sam Snead and Gardner Dickinson, was a success, but the second, in 1979, with its memorable playoff, really sparked the explosion of senior golf. The teams were Roberto De Vicenzo, 56, and Julius Boros, 59, against Tommy Bolt, 61, and Art Wall, 55. Due to a birdie by Boros at the end of regulation, they were set for a playoff.

The teams were well matched—neither gained an advantage on the first four playoff holes, scoring birdie after birdie. Finally, on the fifth playoff hole, Wall and Bolt missed birdie tries while De Vicenzo rolled in his fifth straight birdie.

The quality of play proved that older golfers still had considerable skills—and that there was an audience eager to watch them. The PGA Tour sponsored two senior events of its own in 1980, and the USGA started the U.S. Senior Open in the same year.

Arnold Palmer, who turned 50 in September 1979, joined the new tour in its inaugural season. By 1990, the Senior PGA Tour was a powerful force in the game, having grown to 42 events and $18 million. It is now known as the Champions Tour.

Roberto De Vicenzo

Chapter Four

Hardly Par for the Course: Surprises in Golf

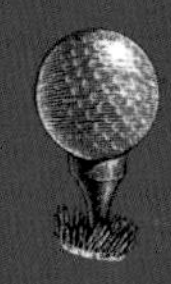

A wealth of factors come into play during any given round, and the unexpected is never far away.

Errant putts are among the most unpleasant surprises in golf.

Ouimet Slays the Giants in Classic U.S. Open

David and two Goliaths? Yes. With slingshot-bearer/caddie Eddie Lowery by his side, frail Francis Ouimet in 1913 vanquished the giants of Britain—sweet-swinging Harry Vardon and burly, pipe-clenching Ted Ray. In the process, golf in America came of age.

Harry Vardon had already built a résumé envied worldwide. Thirteen years earlier, he had come to the States and crushed the opposition in the Open—no American contender even came close. Ray was no slouch either, winning the British Open in 1912 and finishing second in 1913.

But 20-year-old Ouimet had an advantage in the 1913 U.S. Open: He knew The Country Club in Brookline, Massachusetts, like the back of his hand. He had learned golf there as a caddie and had honed his game over the course as an amateur. However, before 1913 he had never even qualified for match play in his own country's amateur championship.

Who can explain what happened? Entering the final round, Vardon, Ray, and Ouimet shared the lead, which didn't change by the end of play. The stage was set, and the playoff began the next day. When it ended, the results were shocking. Ouimet's steady round of 72 prevailed over Vardon's 77 and Ray's 78. It was a giant step for golf in America.

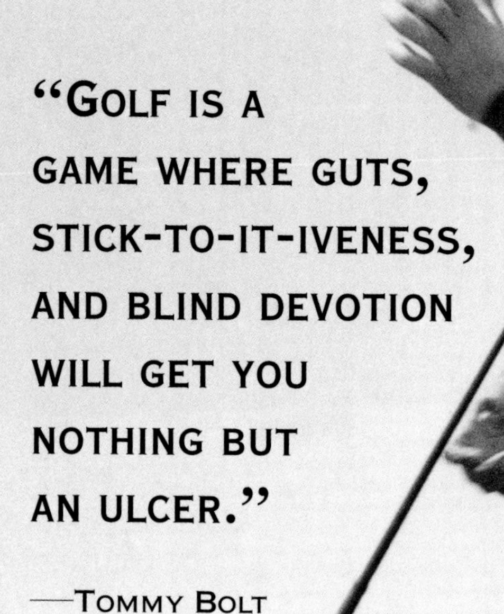

"GOLF IS A GAME WHERE GUTS, STICK-TO-IT-IVENESS, AND BLIND DEVOTION WILL GET YOU NOTHING BUT AN ULCER."

—TOMMY BOLT

The Head Banger

Ivan Gantz had no success as a Tour player in the 1950s, but he became a kind of underground legend because of his outrageous temper. His most bizarre act of anger was, after missing a crucial putt, to whack himself in the head with his putter.

"Actually, that happened a few times," Gantz once recalled, going on to describe one incident in particular. "I was playing on the Tour in Houston, at Memorial Park, and missed a short putt on the last green that would have given me a 68. Man, I raised that putter up and knocked myself in the head with it. I made a pretty good chunk in there, but I didn't fall down, and I wasn't knocked cold, like a lot of people said. People exaggerate."

Parks Comes Out of Nowhere to Win U.S. Open

In 1935, Sam Parks, Jr., became one of the most unlikely and unexpected winners of the U.S. Open when he took the title at the Oakmont Country Club. Parks had been playing the PGA Tour, but his only victory before the Open was in the Western Pennsylvania Junior. Sam was a member of Oakmont, and his local knowledge held him in good stead.

Parks receives his trophy from the president of the United States Golf Association, Prescott Bush.

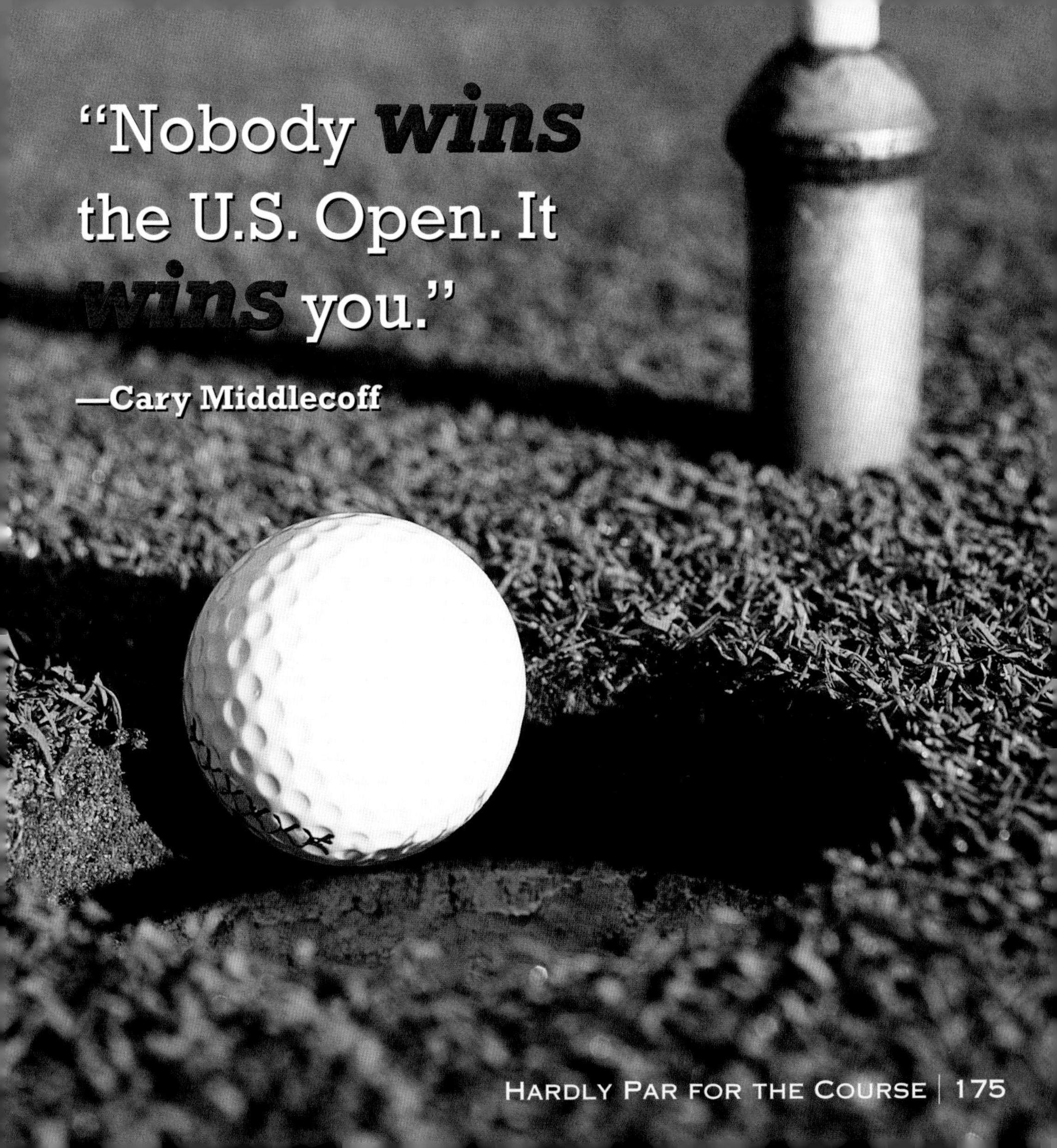

"Nobody **wins** the U.S. Open. It **wins** you."

—Cary Middlecoff

What a Dump!

In 1946, Sam Snead was talked into entering the British Open, being played on the famed Old Course at St. Andrews. Snead had never played in the championship, and this was his first visit to Scotland. While driving along the periphery of the course on his way to his hotel, Snead looked over and saw the hallowed ground. His reaction, however, was rather sacrilegious (although he didn't know it at that moment) when he said to his friend and manager, Fred Corcoran, "Freddie, that looks like an old, abandoned golf course." Be that as it may, Snead won the championship.

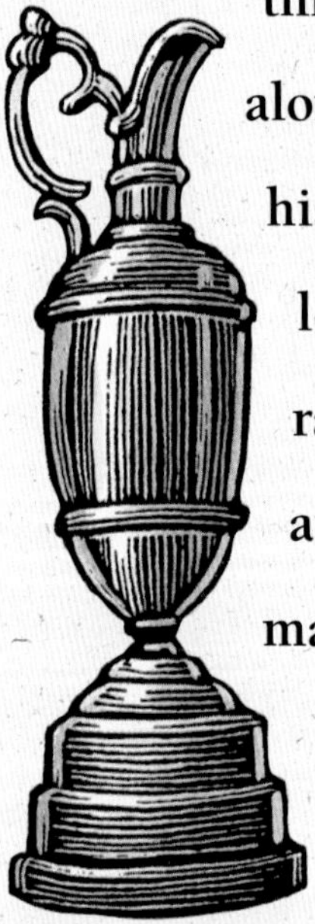

Ballesteros Wins British for First Major Title

Seve Ballesteros, age 22, captured his first major championship by winning the 1979 British Open, at Royal Lytham & St. Annes in England. Seve's 283 beat Jack Nicklaus and Ben Crenshaw by three strokes. On the 70th hole, Ballesteros hit a wild tee shot into a nearby parking lot, yet he reached the green in regulation and wound up birdieing the hole.

Best U.S. Opens

1913: Ouimet's Surprise

Amateur Francis Ouimet needed to play the last six holes at 2-under in the pouring rain to tie Englishmen Harry Vardon and Ted Ray, and he did it. In the next day's 18-hole playoff, Ouimet became the first amateur to claim the U.S. Open.

Arnold Palmer points to his winning score at the 1960 U.S. Open. He had entered the final round seven shots behind.

1950: The Comeback

When Ben Hogan claimed the Open in 1948, he was clearly the best player in the game. The next February, however, he suffered serious injuries in a horrific car crash. Still, he tied Lloyd Mangrum and George Fazio after four rounds and was relentless in the playoff to pull off a dramatic comeback.

1960: Palmer's Charge

Mike Souchak led through each of the first three rounds. Seven others flirted with the lead in the final round before

Jack Nicklaus, a 20-year-old amateur, grabbed it after nine holes, but he couldn't hold it. Ben Hogan was tied for the lead, but he hit into the water on the 17th and 18th. In the end, the Open belonged to Arnold Palmer, who'd entered the final round seven strokes off the lead.

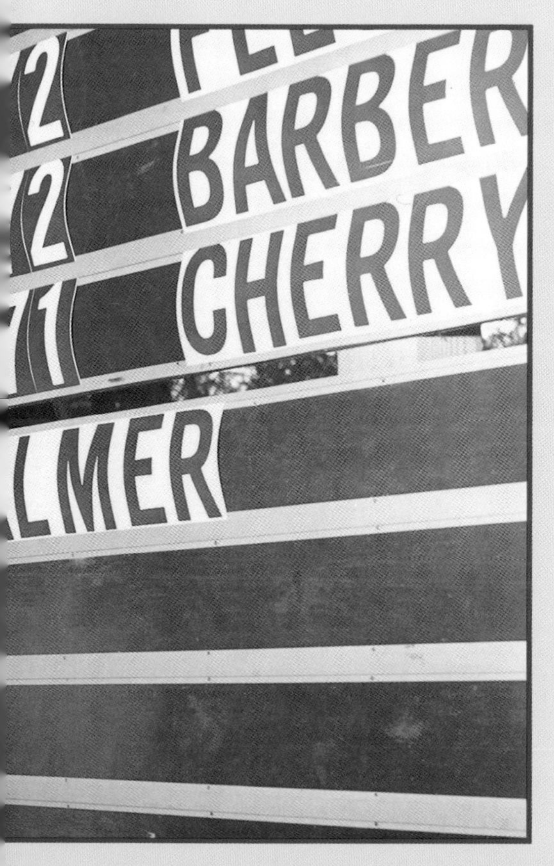

1999: Stewart's Swan Song

For Payne Stewart, it all came down to a 15-foot par putt on the 18th hole of the final round. Phil Mickelson, one back, waited to see if he would make a playoff. Stewart drilled his putt into the center of the hole, the longest putt ever made on the final green to win a U.S. Open by one stroke. It would be his last victory—four months later, he died in a plane crash.

2000: Total Domination

Tiger Woods set the record for margin of victory in a major championship at 15 strokes, breaking the previous mark of 13 set by Old Tom Morris in 1862 when championship golf was in its infancy.

"When he's on," said Ernie Els, who tied for second, "we don't have much of a chance."

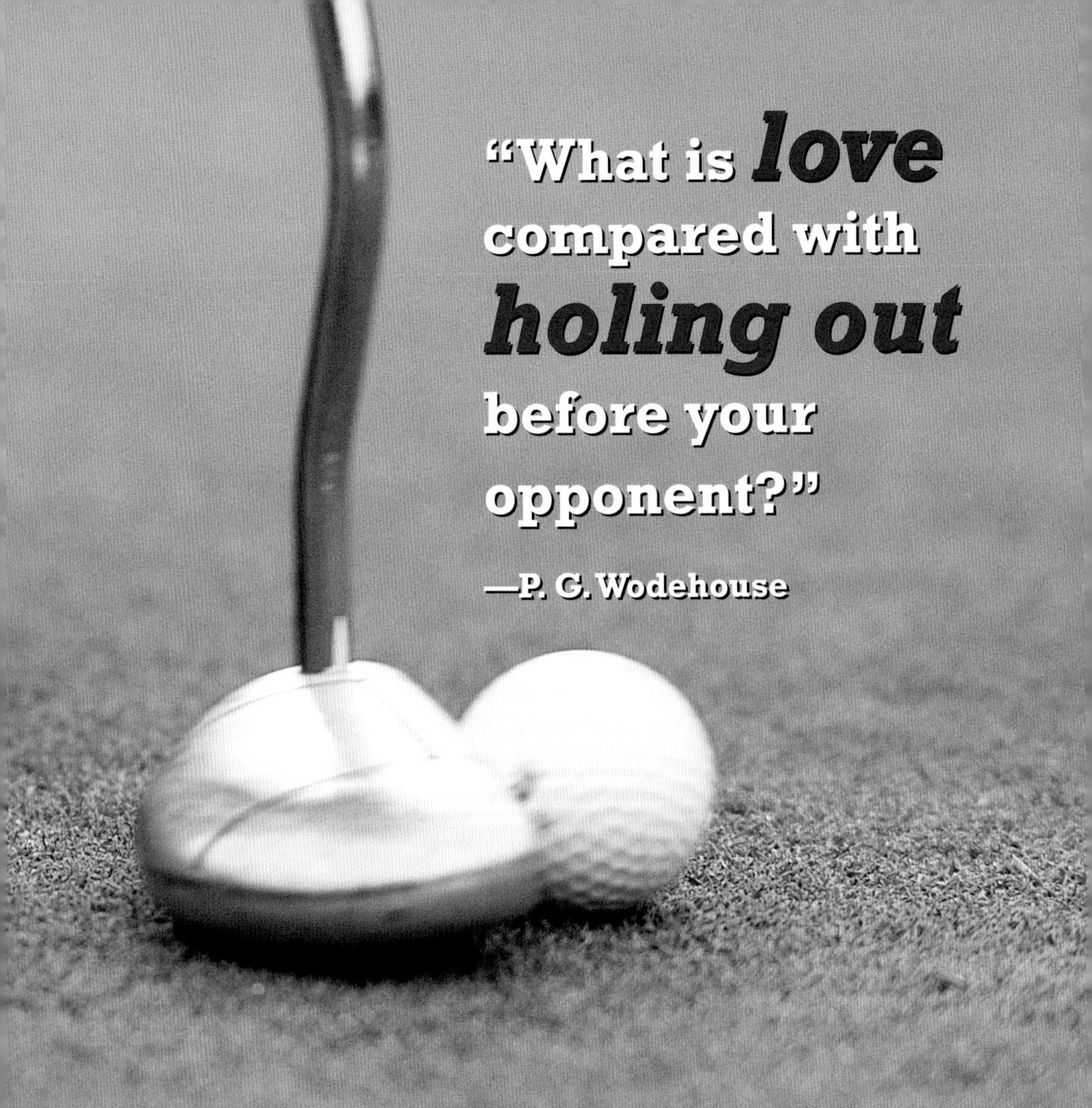
"What is *love* compared with *holing out* before your opponent?"
—P. G. Wodehouse

Four Golfers Ace the 6th Hole at U.S. Open

At the 1989 U.S. Open, four golfers scored a hole-in-one in one day—and on the same hole! Doug Weaver, Jerry Pate, Nick Price, and Mark Wiebe *(left to right)* aced the 159-yard 6th hole in the second round at Oak Hill Country Club. According to the National Hole-in-One Association, the odds of four pros acing the same hole on the same day were 8.7-million-to-1.

A Third-Round Knockout

Bobby Cruickshank was leading after two rounds of the 1934 U.S. Open at the Merion Golf Club, and he was holding on well when in the third round he came to the 11th. His 7-iron approach was a bit on the weak side. The ball descended into the brook in front of the green, but incredibly it landed on a rock and bounced onto the putting surface. Elated, Cruickshank threw his club into the air, shouting, "Thank you, Lord!"

As soon as the words left his mouth, Bobby was knocked in the head by the falling club and felled by the blow. His playing partner, Wiffy Cox, reacted as a boxing referee and began to count Bobby out—they had a sense of humor in those days. Cruickshank was so shaken up that he finished the round with a 77, then shot a 76 in the final round to finish two strokes off the winning pace.

Goodman Becomes Last Amateur to Win Open

Johnny Goodman scored a shocking upset when he defeated Bobby Jones in the first round of the 1929 U.S. Amateur. But Goodman's greatest achievement was his victory in the 1933 U.S. Open, in which he won by a stroke over Ralph Guldahl at North Shore Country Club in Glenview, Illinois. Goodman became the fifth and last amateur to win this title.

Player extended his career thanks to a healthy diet and regular exercise. He proudly points out that he won what he terms the "Senior Grand Slam"—U.S. Senior Open, PGA Seniors Championship, Senior Players Championship, and British Senior Open.

Fitness, practice, and positive thinking were lifelong pursuits for Player. The "Man in Black" maintained his body in peak condition, abstaining from alcohol, tobacco, coffee, tea, sugar, and fried foods, and working incessantly on his game.

Gary Player

Gary Jim Player of Johannesburg, South Africa, seemed no bigger than a jockey compared to most of the golfers he outplayed in winning every major championship in the game at least once. He is one of only five to have done so, joining Gene Sarazen, Ben Hogan, Jack Nicklaus, and Tiger Woods.

Early on, Player had an unorthodox and rather bizarre golf swing, in large part to hit the ball as hard as possible to make up for his size. Altering his overly strong grip and long and complicated swing, he almost immediately began his rise to the top of the heap. Recognizing that the U.S. PGA Tour was the ultimate proving ground for big-time golf, Player began traveling regularly in 1957 to play in the United States. In limited play on the U.S. circuit the next year, he finished in the top 10 ten times, including second place in the U.S. Open.

In 1959, Player won the first of the three British Opens he would capture. In 1961, he won three times on the U.S. Tour, including his first Masters, becoming the first foreign player to win that championship.

Player's reputation grew to such an extent that he, Arnold Palmer, and Nicklaus were considered golf's "Big Three." Player won 24 times on the PGA Tour, including two PGA Championships (1962 and 1972), two more Masters (1974 and 1978), two more British Opens (1968 and 1974), and a U.S. Open (1965). He also won the Australian Open seven times and the World Match Play championship five times and was twice the individual winner of the World Cup. On the Champions Tour, Player won 19 times from 1985 to 1998.

Holy Smokes! Fleck Upsets Hogan in U.S. Open

In one of golf's greatest upsets, Jack Fleck beat Ben Hogan in a playoff for the 1955 U.S. Open crown. Hogan, here fanning Fleck's hot putter, was unable to match the Davenport, Iowa, professional on the greens. Fleck's putting was boldly accurate, and he fired a 69 to Hogan's 72. The world of golf was stunned.

“My favourite shots are the *practice swing* and the *conceded putt*.”

**—Lord Robertson,
former secretary general of NATO**

"It's good sportsmanship not to pick up lost golf balls while they are still rolling."

—Mark Twain

Journeyman Hamilton Stuns Nelson in PGA

Bob Hamilton, a pro from Indiana with a thin résumé, surprised the golf world by reaching the finals of the 1944 PGA Championship, then defeating Byron Nelson for the title. Hamilton was a 10–1 underdog going into the match, but he seemed unfazed as he made one fine swing after another and won, 1 up.

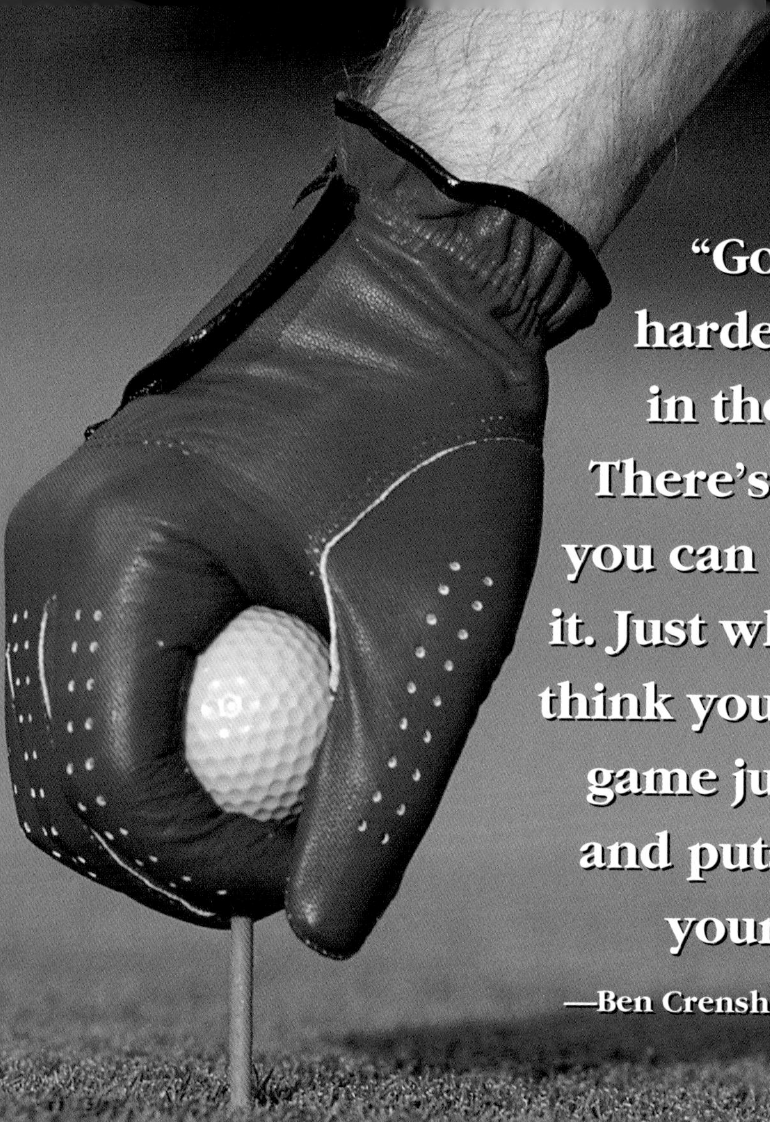

"Golf is the hardest game in the world. There's no way you can ever get it. Just when you think you do, the game jumps up and puts you in your place."

—Ben Crenshaw, *Golf Talk*

Amateur Lacoste Prevails in Women's Open

Catherine Lacoste became the first amateur to win the U.S. Women's Open with her victory in the 1967 championship, at the Virginia Hot Springs Golf and Tennis Club. She won by two strokes despite closing with a 79. Lacoste, of Paris, France, was the daughter of tennis great Rene Lacoste.

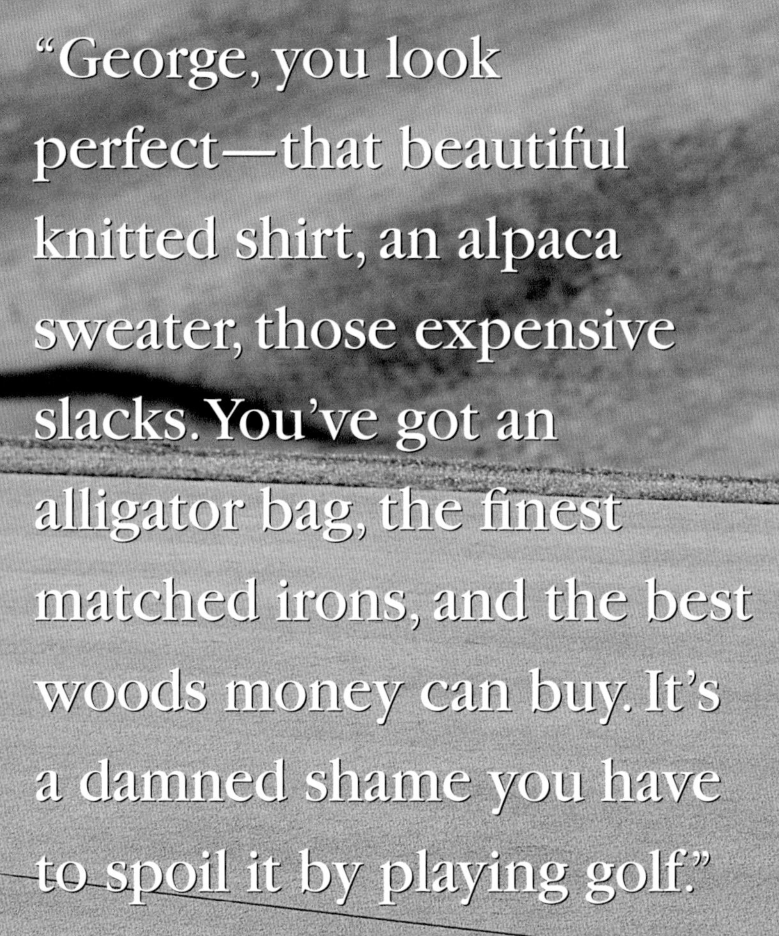

"George, you look perfect—that beautiful knitted shirt, an alpaca sweater, those expensive slacks. You've got an alligator bag, the finest matched irons, and the best woods money can buy. It's a damned shame you have to spoil it by playing golf."

—Lloyd Mangrum, to comedian George Burns

Europe Claims First Cup on American Soil

The 1987 European Ryder Cup team, led by captain Tony Jacklin *(holding trophy)*, repeated its 1985 victory by barely edging a frustrated U.S. squad, 15–13. It was only the second time in 30 years that the United States had lost, and it was its first loss ever on American soil. Seve Ballesteros led Europe with four points.

Tom Kite

Kite's breakthrough year came in 1981, with a phenomenal 21 top-10 finishes in 26 starts.

With the exception of 1988, he won at least one tournament in every year from 1981 to 1993 for a career total of 19 victories.

He topped the money list in 1981 and 1989.

Although he earned more than $10 million in over a quarter-century on Tour, Kite always viewed golf more as a recreation than an occupation.

"Golf has never been work for me. You don't work golf. You play it."

"Nothing goes **down** slower than a golf ***handicap***."

—Bobby Nichols

"No, sir. We couldn't 'ave a coincidence like that."

—Scottish caddie,
on being told he was the worst caddie in the world

The $50-Million Shot

In 1987 in Benin, West Africa, a factory overseer, Mathieu Boya, decided to spend his lunch break practicing his shot-making. The improvised range was an area adjacent to the country's main air base. One errant shot sliced over the fence, hitting a bird. The bird plunged through the windshield of a jet in the process of taking off. While the pilot tried to gain control of the plane, he had little luck, and it crashed into four other jets parked on the runway.

In effect, it destroyed Benin's entire air force.

The police arrested Boya, presenting him with a bill for about $50 million, give or take a few million. He was charged with "hooliganism" and sent to prison.

Tiny McLeod Plays Big in U.S. Open Playoff

Fred McLeod, shown here later in life, was a wisp of a man at 108 pounds when he won the 1908 U.S. Open at Myopia Hunt Club in Massachusetts. McLeod tied Willie Smith with a bloated score of 322, then downed him in an 18-hole playoff, 77–83. McLeod would never again win the Open, but he'd finish a shot out of a playoff in both 1910 and 1911.

Benepe Wins the Western, His First Tour Event

Jim Benepe turned more than a few heads when he won the 1988 Beatrice Western Open. Amazingly, Benepe had never played in a PGA Tour event before, and he snuck into this one only because he was given a sponsor's exemption. Benepe led the Canadian Tour's Order of Merit in 1987.

Venturi Beats the Heat, Wins U.S. Open

On the 72nd green of the 1964 U.S. Open at Congressional Country Club in Bethesda, Maryland, Ken Venturi looked awful. He was tired and sweaty. Yet he lined up a 10-foot putt and knocked it into the hole. "My God!" he yelled. "I won the Open."

In those days, the final two rounds of the Open were played on Saturday, and on this Saturday, the temperature soared to 100 degrees. Six strokes behind the leader, Venturi got off to a surprising start in the third round. His 10-foot birdie putt on the 1st hole initially stopped on the lip, yet as he walked up to the ball, it dropped in.

Venturi had four more front-nine birdies for a 30 and was 6-under-par until the 17th hole, when he sat on the edge of his bag suffering from the heat. He bogied 17 and 18 but still shot 66. Venturi staggered into the clubhouse, where Dr. John Everett noticed the golfer was suffering from heat prostration. He gave him some tea and salt tablets.

As the fourth round began, Dr. Everett followed Venturi with a wet towel. Surprisingly, Venturi was still playing well. His 18-foot birdie putt on 13 pumped him up. He stepped onto the 18th tee four strokes ahead of the field.

Venturi sunk that 10-footer for par and a 70. He went on to win two more 1964 tournaments and become the Player of the Year.

No Putts in a Round

Canadian Murray "Moe" Norman had an outstanding record in his native country: He won 54 amateur and professional tournaments and made a brief stab at the PGA Tour. Moe held 33 course records, 17 of them being set the first time he had ever seen the course. The Royal Canadian Golf Association inducted him into its Hall of Fame in 1995.

In the 1969 Quebec Open, Norman came to the final hole needing a birdie to win outright and a par to get in a playoff. Moe hit the par-5 in two and proceeded to four-putt. The next day, on the par-3 10th hole of a practice round, some writers asked him about his putting. Moe didn't answer until he hit his shot. While it was still in the air, he said, "I'm not putting today." The shot went straight into the cup for a hole-in-one.

Baker Enjoys Day of Fame at U.S. Women's Open

Kathy Baker, the 1982 national collegiate champion, proved the victor in the 1985 U.S. Women's Open, at Baltusrol Golf Club in Springfield, New Jersey. Baker won by three strokes over runner-up Judy Clark. It was the only time Baker won or finished runner-up in a major championship; in fact, she won only one more LPGA Tour event.

Bing's Son Nate Wins Dramatic U.S. Amateur

Nathaniel Crosby hugs his mom, Kathryn Crosby, widow of actor Bing Crosby. Nate, age 19, won the 1981 U.S. Amateur at the Olympic Country Club in San Francisco, 15 miles from the Crosby home. In a thrilling finale, he beat Brian Lindley, 1 up in 37 holes. Crosby won it by holing a 20-foot birdie putt on the first extra hole.

Swedish Rookie Neumann Wins U.S. Women's Open

Sweden's Liselotte Neumann proved herself in America with her first LPGA Tour victory, the 1988 U.S. Women's Open. On the Five Farms Course at Baltimore Country Club, Neumann outlasted Patty Sheehan to win by three strokes. Though a rookie on the LPGA Tour, Neumann excelled in Europe the three previous years.

Amateur Riley Wins First-Ever LPGA Event

Polly Riley of Fort Worth, Texas, stunned the touring pros by winning the 1950 Tampa Women's Open. The Tampa Open, the first official event of the new Ladies Professional Golf Association, was designed to showcase the women pros. Riley, an amateur, added insult to injury by shooting 295, tying the tournament record.

Miller Breaks from the Booth and Beats Watson in Pro-Am

Johnny Miller shocked everyone, including himself, when he won the AT&T Pebble Beach National Pro-Am in 1994 at age 46, beating 44-year-old Tom Watson in a battle of old folks. Miller had retired from the Tour a few years earlier, entering only one or two events a year while concentrating on his broadcasting role at NBC.

Chapter Five

Rounding Out the Field:

Golf Miscellanea

The breadth and depth of the game encompasses a wide variety of people, places, and subjects.

Spectators crowd the 16th hole at Augusta National during the 1991 Masters.

Kathy Whitworth

In a society with the collective attention span the length of a television commercial, Kathy Whitworth's career may not seem noteworthy. But for those who understand and appreciate the strength involved in upholding a well-honed athletic talent—and the determination to maintain a high standard for more than four decades—Whitworth will always be reassuring.

Kathrynne Ann Whitworth took up golf at 15 and turned pro at 19. She seemed set to light up the women's golf world right from the start, but her fuse was a slow one. In her first season, 1959, she entered 26 events and won a total of $1,217.

In 1962, Whitworth won her first LPGA tournament, the Kelly Girl Open. In 28 appearances that year, she won enough money to reach five figures for the first time—$17,044.

In 1963, Whitworth won eight tournaments. After only one victory in 1964, she won eight more times in 1965, including her first major, the Titleholders Championship. In 1967, she won eight events including two majors—the LPGA Championship and the Western Open. Throughout her career, she won 88 Tour events, more than any other pro golfer, male or female.

Whitworth was the leading money winner on the LPGA circuit eight times and won the Vare Trophy (for low stroke average) seven times. She became the first woman to reach $1 million in career prize money. Many consider her the greatest woman golfer of modern times.

Glen Abbey

The 18th hole at Glen Abbey, which hosts the Bell Canadian Open, is one of the top finishing holes on the PGA Tour. The 508-yard par-5 is short enough for long hitters to go for the green in two. But those daring souls must contend with a large pond that fronts the right side of the green. The best line off the tee is to aim left center, hugging the four fairway bunkers on that side. The tree-lined approach must work its way between the water on the right and two bunkers left of the green. Laying up short of the putting surface is the more advisable route for most golfers.

"Golf: A game in which you claim the privileges of age, and retain the playthings of childhood."

—Samuel Johnson

David Mulligan's Do-Over

In the late 1920s, four golfers played fairly regularly at St. Lambert Country Club near Montreal. One of them had an automobile, and it was his job to drive to the course with the other members of the group. The route included driving over a bridge with cross ties, constructed that way to take care of horse-drawn wagons.

They would rush to the tee upon arrival, but the driver, shaken by crossing the bridge, usually hit a poor shot. Since he was the only one with an automobile, it was a common practice to allow him to hit a second tee shot. After all, they didn't want to lose their transportation. The golfer's name was David Mulligan, manager of the Windsor Hotel in Montreal, and the act of hitting a second shot off the 1st tee became known as "hitting a Mulligan."

Japanese Taboos

If you're playing golf in Japan, chances are pretty good you won't run into someone using a golf ball with the number 4 on it. That's a bad-luck number for the Japanese, and they do not manufacture any for the locals. Instead, a dozen Japanese balls are numbered 1, 2, 3, and 7.

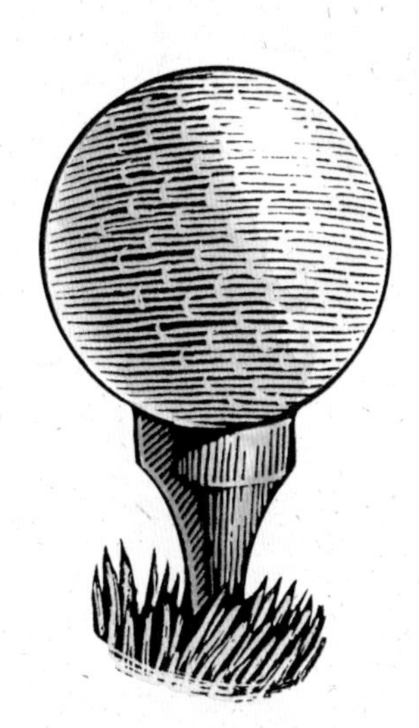

"I don't like *No. 4* balls. And I don't like *5s*, *6s*, or *7s* on my scorecard."

—George Archer

"Golf has drawbacks.
It is possible, by too much of it,
to destroy the mind."

—Sir Walter Simpson

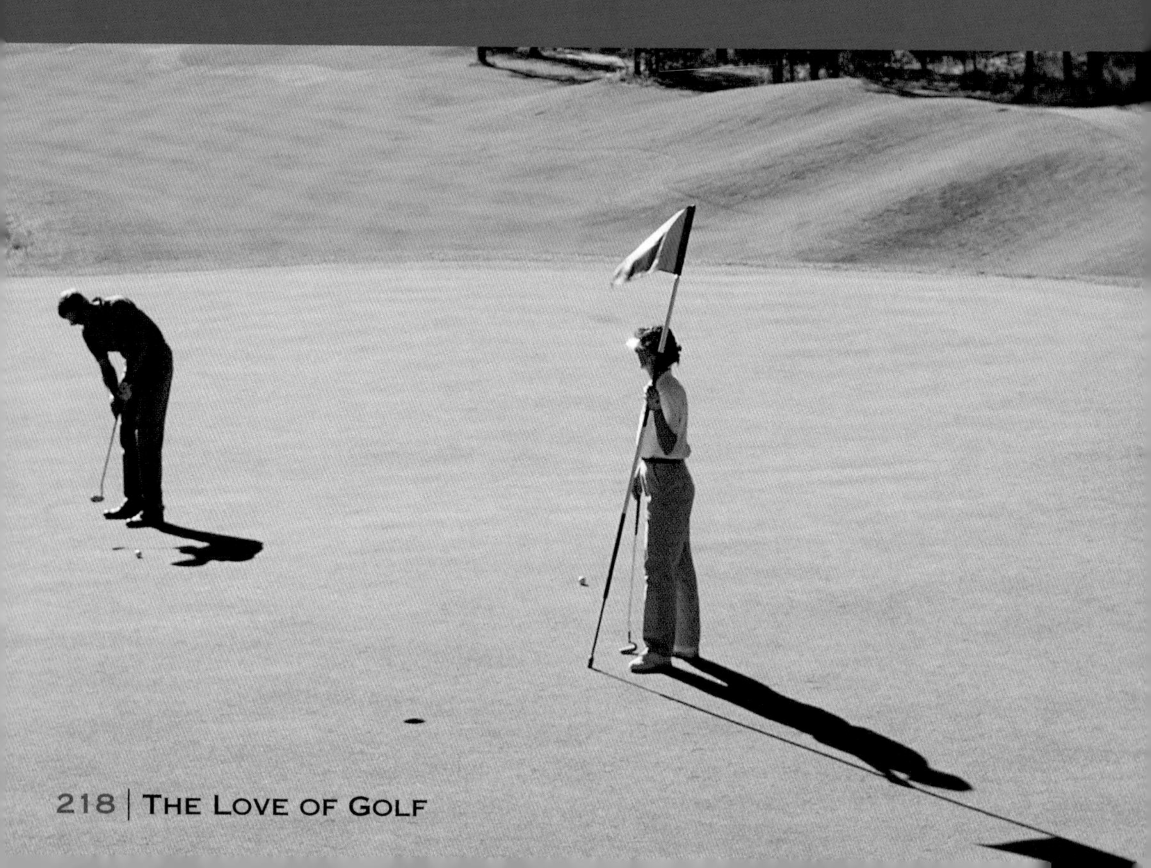

Fans Live on the Edge at Pebble Beach

The 8th hole at Pebble Beach Golf Links has always been a treacherous one—especially in the early days, when spectators were just a slippery spot away from plunging to their death. Rocky cliffs line the entire right side of the par-4 8th hole. The approach shot must carry both ocean and rocks to reach the green.

Best U.S. Holes

▼ Augusta National 12th

The shortest par-3 on the course, the 12th has never yielded a below-par average score during the Masters tournament. Rae's Creek runs in front of the green with Ben Hogan Bridge providing a way across the water.

Baltusrol (Lower) 17th

Jack Nicklaus called this one of the great par-5 holes in America. It stretches to a gargantuan 647 yards from the back tees. The golfer must hit a solid drive and an excellent second shot to make it across The Sahara, an

enormous bunker crossing the fairway at 420 yards.

Cypress Point 16th

The tee and green of the 233-yard par-3 16th sit precariously close to the Monterey Peninsula's ocean cliffs. In between is an awe-inspiring ocean inlet. From the back tee, the drive must carry 220 yards to clear the cliffs on line with the green.

Merion (East) 16th

Lying in the heart of what many consider the toughest five finishing holes in golf, this par-4 plays 428 yards from the back tees. The approach must carry at least 120 yards across an abandoned rock quarry shared with the 17th hole.

Pinehurst (No. 2) 5th

This is a 482-yard par-4 with a blind landing area that falls off to the left. A drive to the left center of the fairway will likely bounce down into the rough, leaving little chance to go for the green. Course architect Donald Ross once called it the hardest second shot in golf.

Southern Hills 12th

Arnold Palmer and Ben Hogan called this 458-yard par-4 the best 12th hole in the country. The golfer must contend with a stream that crosses in front of the green, disappears briefly underground, and then reemerges up the right side of the putting surface.

"THE *GAME* WAS EASY FOR ME AS A KID, AND I HAD TO PLAY A WHILE TO FIND OUT HOW *HARD* IT IS."

—RAYMOND FLOYD

Lind Tops Venturi in First Junior Amateur

In 1948, 17-year-old Dean Lind *(right)*, of Rockford, Illinois, defeated Ken Venturi *(left)* to win the first edition of the U.S. Junior Amateur championship. Lind beat Venturi, a San Francisco junior, 4 & 2, in the final. Venturi was somewhat hampered by a sore back. The first Junior Amateur attracted 495 contestants.

Billy Casper

It's difficult to say just why Billy Casper was never recognized for the golfer he was. It may have been the way he presented himself to the golfing public. Perhaps, too, it was because he defeated one of the game's most beloved icons, Arnold Palmer, for a national championship.

From 1954, when he turned pro, through 1979, his last year on the regular PGA Tour, Casper won 51 tournaments to place sixth on the all-time winners list. His victories included two U.S. Opens (1959 and 1966) and a Masters (1970). He played on eight U.S. Ryder Cup teams, was a nonplaying captain for one other, and won the annual Vardon Trophy for low stroke average five times. He was twice the Tour's leading money winner, and in 1970 he became the second golfer in history to win more than $1 million in career prize money. Twice PGA Player of the Year, he is a member of the PGA/World Golf Hall of Fame. By all accounts, he was one of the best players in American golf history.

Casper said he would have been more popular had he not tried to emulate the unemotional, stoic Ben Hogan. But his cardinal sin, as many seemed to consider it, occurred in 1966. With nine holes to play in that year's U.S. Open, held at the Olympic Club in San Francisco, Casper came from seven strokes behind to tie Palmer. Then, in the 18-hole playoff, Casper erased a two-stroke deficit with eight holes to play for the title itself, his second. Had he defeated anyone besides the popular Palmer, Casper might have been extolled more for his achievement. In a sense, he was a victim of someone else's charisma.

Casper Rattles Off Three Consecutive Victories

Billy Casper had many opportunities to give the victory salute in the 1960s. Matching Arnold Palmer's feat of that spring, Casper won three straight PGA Tour tournaments in 1960. Billy's victories came in the early fall and included the Portland Open, Hesperia Open, and Orange County Open.

Keiser Prevails in Masters—By That Much

Herman Keiser (*center*) won his only major championship when he captured the 1946 Masters, after Ben Hogan missed a 30-inch putt on the final hole. Hogan shows Keiser and tournament host Bobby Jones the size of his missed putt.

Cypress Point

Mix in one part world's greatest architect (Alister Mackenzie) and one part world's greatest golf site (Monterey Peninsula), and what you get is Cypress Point Club, considered by many the best golf course in the world. Mackenzie, architect of such renowned layouts as Augusta National and Royal Melbourne, had the good sense to let the land dictate the layout at Cypress Point.

The course includes back-to-back par-3s, par-5s, and short par-4s. But despite the unusual sequencing, the holes lay perfectly over the windswept woods, hillsides, links, and cliffs that make up the spectacular Monterey Peninsula.

The 233-yard, par-3 16th, pictured here, may be the most photographed and most strategic hole in the world. From a tee hugging the Pacific, the stout of heart take aim directly at a green backed by the ocean. The carry is some 220 yards across pounding surf 100 feet below. There is also a bail-out area left of the green, leaving a chance for a skillful up and down (but more likely a bogey).

The 15th is another ocean-side par-3. It is a much shorter shot, a pitching wedge to the green. The dogleg, par-4 17th sits astride the Pacific—the tee shot must cross the water to a fairway split in two by a stand of cypress trees. The green is barely visible past the trees and cliffs that mark the landing area. While the rest of the course has many spectacular holes, the 15–17 stretch makes for one of the most dramatic climaxes to any round of golf.

When asked to compare Cypress Point to nearby Pebble Beach Golf Links, the legendary Bobby Jones replied: "Pebble Beach is more difficult, but Cypress is more fun."

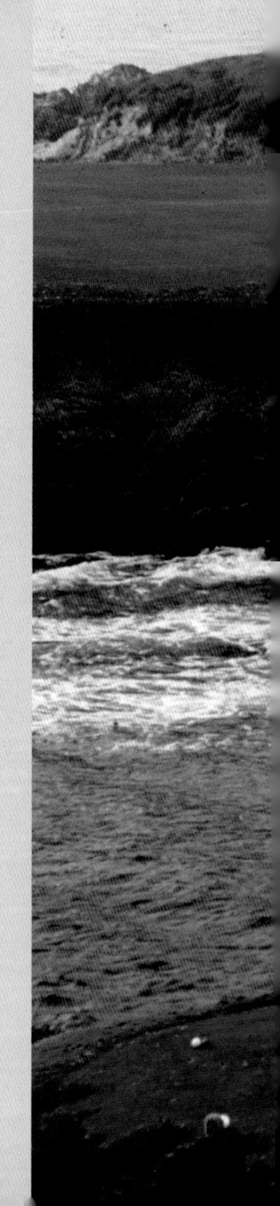

Cary Middlecoff

Walter Hagen called Cary Middlecoff one of the best ball-strikers to come out of American golf.

Middlecoff won two U.S. Opens (1949 and 1956), losing another in a playoff (1957), and won one Masters title (1955), with two seconds at Augusta National.

The son of a dentist, Middlecoff shared his father's practice before taking up professional golf.

One of the more deliberate players in the game, Middlecoff fidgeted over the ball at address for some time before beginning his swing. Dan Jenkins wrote, "A joke on the Tour used to be that Cary gave up dentistry because no patient could keep his mouth open that long."

With 40 wins from 1945 to 1961, Middlecoff is in the top ten for all-time Tour wins.

In 1951, Middlecoff joined an elite group of golfers in winning three consecutive events.

Shoot the Lowest Score

In 1994, Nick Faldo had a chance to meet the reclusive, famously terse Ben Hogan. Faldo had by then won the Masters twice and the British Open three times but had yet to capture a U.S. Open. Hogan had won it four times, so Faldo wanted insight about how he might, as well.

Nick Faldo

Faldo asked, "How do you win the U.S. Open?" Hogan looked across his desk with his steely blue eyes fixed on Faldo and responded, ***"Shoot the lowest score."*** Faldo thought Hogan was kidding and asked again, "No really, Mr. Hogan, how do you win the U.S. Open?" Hogan sat upright in his chair, leaned toward the young Briton, and gave him the notorious Hogan glare as he repeated his original answer: ***"Shoot the lowest score."*** With that, Hogan turned away. The interview was concluded. Faldo, baffled, rose and left shaking his head at this no-frills advice. Hogan was not one for frills.

Ben Hogan

Cooper Comes Up Short Again

When Harry Cooper (*pictured)* was edged out by Horton Smith in the 1936 Masters, he said to Bobby Jones: "It seems that it was not intended for me to ever win a major tournament." His prophecy was fulfilled later that year when he set a new scoring record for the U.S. Open only to have it broken a half-hour later by Tony Manero, the tournament's winner. Cooper never won a major.

Best PGA Championships

1923:
The Kid Tops the Haig

Gene Sarazen faced Walter Hagen in a playoff after the 36-hole final ended up tied. On the second hole, a short par-4, Hagen hit near the green, Sarazen into the rough. Reportedly telling the gallery, "I'll put this one up so close to the hole that it will break Walter's heart," Sarazen played a marvelous shot that stopped two feet from the flagstick. After a startled Hagen flubbed a short pitch, Sarazen putted to victory.

1940:
Lord Byron

Byron Nelson led for most of the 36-hole match at Hershey Country Club in Pennsylvania, but Sam Snead rallied on the back nine, birdieing the 12th, 13th, and 14th holes to take a 1-up lead. After both parred the 15th, Nelson unleashed a trio of near-perfect iron shots to break Snead's momentum and claim the match.

1978:
Mahaffey's Comeback

Tom Watson, the best in the world at the time, led by four at the turn in the final round. But his last few holes included a bogey and a double bogey, which allowed a tie with Jerry Pate and John Mahaffey, whose closing 66 had made up seven strokes on Watson. When Mahaffey won on the

second hole of the sudden-death playoff, he achieved the best come-back in PGA Championship history.

◀ 2000: A Triple Crown

Tiger Woods had won 2000's U.S. and British Opens. A win here would match Ben Hogan (1953) as the only player to win three professional majors in one year. Not as sharp as he might have been, Woods headed to the last nine tied with Bob May. Playing together, each produced a 5-under-par 31, with Woods holing clutch putt after clutch putt. On the first hole of a three-hole playoff, Woods sank a 20-footer for a birdie, giving him a one-stroke lead and sending him to victory.

"It is almost impossible to remember how tragic a place the world is when one is playing golf."

—Robert Lynd

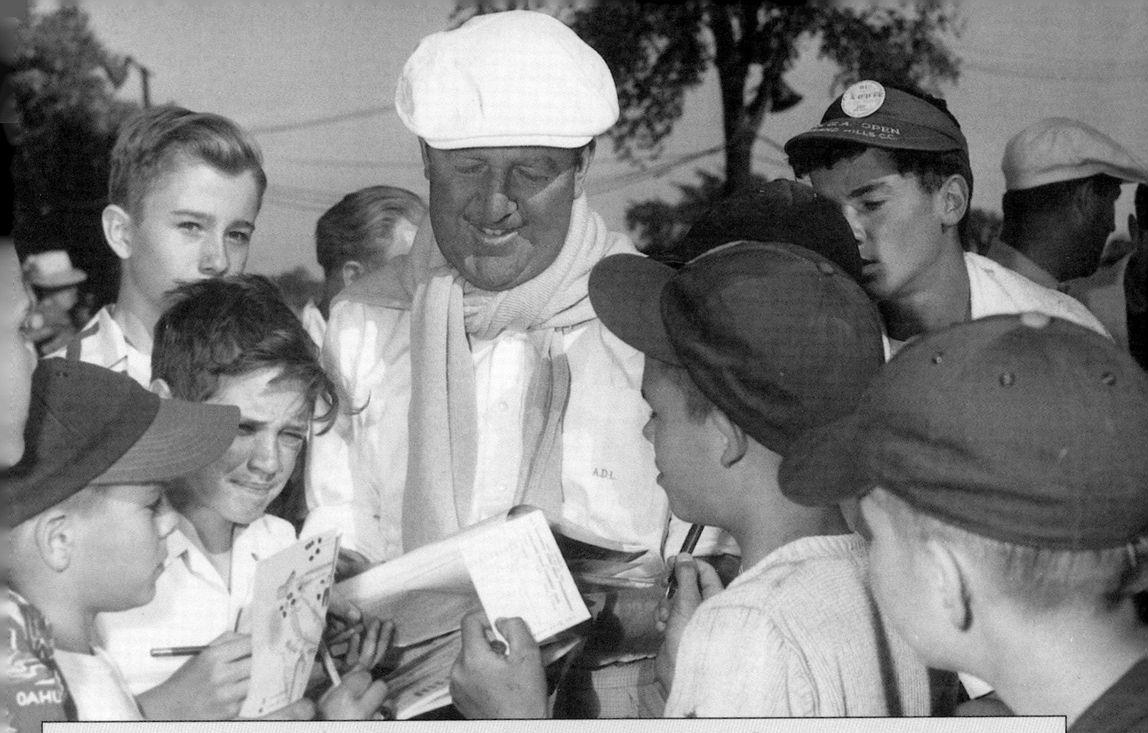

Locke's Hot Putter Leads to 16-Stroke Victory

Bobby Locke, perhaps golf's greatest putter, signs autographs for youngsters after one-putting nine greens at Chicago's Midlothian Country Club for a blistering 65 in the 1948 Chicago Victory Open. The South African won the tournament by 16 strokes—a margin that's never been bettered on the PGA Tour.

JoAnne Carner

Of the great players to come along in the post-World War II era, JoAnne Carner is the only one, male or female, who nearly remained a career amateur. Not turning pro until age 30, Carner won five U.S. Women's Amateur championships, a total second to only Glenna Collett Vare. As a pro, she compiled a record that placed her in the LPGA Hall of Fame.

Carner, née Gunderson, is the only player to have claimed the U.S. Girls' Junior, Women's Amateur, and Women's Open titles. She took the amateur title in 1957, 1960, 1962, 1966, and 1968. In 1969, she won the Burdine's Invitational on the LPGA Tour; she remains the last amateur to win an LPGA event.

With prize money rising in the pro game and no worlds left to conquer in amateur golf, Carner turned pro in 1970. The former "Great Gundy" earned a new nickname on Tour when her fellow pros tabbed her "Big Momma," mainly for her ability to launch the ball long distances. Carner's gregarious personality and go-for-broke style made her a popular figure in the pro ranks.

Carner's impressive Tour record included winning the Vare Trophy for low scoring average five times, earning three Player of the Year Awards, and claiming three money titles. Her biggest victories came in the 1971 and 1976 U.S. Women's Opens. From 1974 to 1983, she ranked among the top five money winners in all but one year. Despite her late start, Carner had a long stay near the top of the LPGA, achieving more success after age 40 than any player of either sex ever has. Of her 42 LPGA Tour victories, 19 came in her 40s, and she led the money list at ages 43 and 44.

"Golf is like a

love affair.

If you don't take it

seriously,

it's not fun. If you take it

too seriously,

it breaks your

heart."

—Arnold Daly

Boxer Louis Takes a Shot at Tam O'Shanter

Heavyweight champion Joe Louis, an avid golfer, was invited to play in the 1943 Tam O'Shanter All-American Amateur tournament in Chicago. Louis, on furlough from the Army, didn't qualify, but he stayed on to play exhibitions to raise money for the War Fund. Here, Louis shakes hands with Byron Nelson.

Best World Holes

Ballybunion (Old) 11th

The 11th hole at this Irish course is among the most compelling holes in the world. Landscape falls away to the blue waters of the Atlantic before dancing along the cliff tops to a landing area bordered by even taller windswept sandhills and the ocean.

Carnoustie 6th

The 578-yard 6th is the longest and best hole at Scotland's Carnoustie. The wide green is protected by deep bunkers front right and rear left.

Royal Melbourne (West) 6th

The 451-yard 6th hole at Australia's Royal Melbourne's West Course mixes strategy with striking natural features. A sharp dogleg-right makes it imperative that the drive carry across dense rough and traps for prime position within an enormous fairway.

Casa de Campo 16th

The 16th is routed along the bright blue waters of the Caribbean at this beautiful Dominican Republic resort. The par-3, 185-yard masterpiece is best played from the back tees.

Muirfield 18th

The 18th hole on this Scottish course may be the world's top finishing hole. The narrow green on the 447-yard hole is embraced by a pair of deep bunkers right and left.

Royal Troon 8th ▶

The 126-yard 8th hole—the "Postage Stamp"—is the shortest par-3 on the British Open circuit but is not without its challenge. The tiny green is surrounded by five deep bunkers.

St. Andrews (Old) 17th

The Road Hole on Scotland's St. Andrews's Old Course may be the

most famous in the game. The drive must cross an out-of-bounds area—formerly the railroad stationmaster's garden—and avoid the roadway that runs up the right side of the fairway.

Turnberry (Ailsa) 9th

The view from the 454-yard 9th tee of Turnberry's Ailsa Course is one of the most stunning and intimidating in golf. From a tee teetering high above the surf, the golfer looks across a carry that drops into a deep abyss.

Valderrama 4th

The 4th hole at Spain's Valderrama is a breathtaking 564-yard par-5. A lake and bunkers guard the right side of the elevated green with a neighboring waterfall.

"There is one essential only in the golf swing: The ball must be hit."

—Sir Walter Simpson

Wethered and the Rumbling Train

Bobby Jones once said that Joyce Wethered was the best golfer, man or woman, he had ever seen. She had the capacity for concentration that is as much the mark of a great champion as swing technique. Wethered exhibited this talent in her first tournament, the 1920 Women's English Championship.

Four down after the first 18 holes, Wethered fought her way back, and when she reached the 17th (35th) hole she was 1 up on the reigning queen of British golf, Cecil Leitch. A railway line ran close to the green where Wethered had a short putt that, if she made it, would close out the match. While a train thundered past, Wethered calmly stroked her ball into the hole to win the title. When asked later why she hadn't waited until the train had passed, she said, with some surprise, "What train?"

Gene Littler

His rhythmic swing and unerring accuracy earned Gene Littler the nickname "Gene the Machine."

Littler's successful career included 29 PGA Tour victories over 23 years.

His best year was 1959 with five victories.

Shooting a final-round 68 and coming from three strokes behind at the 1961 U.S. Open at Oakland Hills gave him the biggest win of his career.

Littler finished out of the top 32 money winners only once from 1954 to 1976. He ranked second on the list in 1959 and 1962.

Annual PGA Money Leaders

Year	Player	Earnings
1934	Paul Runyan	$6,767
1935	Johnny Revolta	9,543
1936	Horton Smith	7,682
1937	Harry Cooper	14,139
1938	Sam Snead	19,534
1939	Henry Picard	10,303
1940	Ben Hogan	10,655
1941	Ben Hogan	18,358
1942	Ben Hogan	13,143
1943	No records kept	
1944	Byron Nelson	37,968
1945	Byron Nelson	63,336
1946	Ben Hogan	42,556
1947	Jimmy Demaret	27,937
1948	Ben Hogan	32,112
1949	Sam Snead	31,594
1950	Sam Snead	35,759
1951	Lloyd Mangrum	26,089
1952	Julius Boros	37,033
1953	Lew Worsham	34,002
1954	Bob Toski	65,820
1955	Julius Boros	63,122
1956	Ted Kroll	72,836
1957	Dick Mayer	65,835
1958	Arnold Palmer	42,608
1959	Art Wall	53,168
1960	Arnold Palmer	75,263
1961	Gary Player	64,540
1962	Arnold Palmer	81,448
1963	Arnold Palmer	128,230
1964	Jack Nicklaus	113,285
1965	Jack Nicklaus	140,752
1966	Billy Casper	121,945
1967	Jack Nicklaus	188,998
1968	Billy Casper	205,169
1969	Frank Beard	164,707
1970	Lee Trevino	157,037
1971	Jack Nicklaus	244,491
1972	Jack Nicklaus	320,542
1973	Jack Nicklaus	308,362
1974	Johnny Miller	353,022
1975	Jack Nicklaus	298,149
1976	Jack Nicklaus	266,439
1977	Tom Watson	310,653
1978	Tom Watson	362,429
1979	Tom Watson	462,636
1980	Tom Watson	530,808
1981	Tom Kite	375,699
1982	Craig Stadler	446,462
1983	Hal Sutton	426,668

1984	Tom Watson	476,260
1985	Curtis Strange	542,321
1986	Greg Norman	653,296
1987	Curtis Strange	925,941
1988	Curtis Strange	1,147,644
1989	Tom Kite	1,395,278
1990	Greg Norman	1,165,477
1991	Corey Pavin	979,430
1992	Fred Couples	1,344,188
1993	Nick Price	1,478,557
1994	Nick Price	1,499,927
1995	Greg Norman	1,654,959
1996	Tom Lehman	1,780,159
1997	Tiger Woods	2,066,833
1998	David Duval	2,591,031
1999	Tiger Woods	6,616,585
2000	Tiger Woods	9,188,321
2001	Tiger Woods	5,687,777
2002	Tiger Woods	6,912,625
2003	Vijay Singh	7,573,907
2004	Vijay Singh	10,905,166

Vijay Singh entered the record books in 2004, becoming the first golfer to win more than $10 million in a single year.

Valderrama

Spain's Valderrama is traditionally voted the top course in continental Europe. The course overlooks the Atlantic Ocean with sweeping views of Gibraltar and North Africa. It has immaculate, lightning-quick bentgrass greens and lush Bermuda grass fairways dressed up with more than 2,000 gnarled old cork trees, some of which predate Christopher Columbus. Olive trees, flower beds, and white-sand bunkers also dot the landscape. The greens and trees, as well as the wind, make Valderrama a thinking person's course. "There are so many shots to be hit here," European star Colin Montgomerie told golf.com.

The 17th was redesigned by Spanish golfer Seve Ballesteros at the suggestion of Robert Trent Jones, Sr. The green on the 536-yarder is fronted by a pond that has absorbed many an approach shot. Tiger Woods doesn't like it. "It's not a very well-designed hole," he said. "And unfortunately, if you just walk around the bank, look how many balls are in the water." But there are few other complaints about Valderrama's layout.

Valderrama President Jaime Ortiz-Patino is a trained superintendent and has made a commitment to both superb conditions and the environment. In addition to constantly being tweaked to improve conditions and challenge, the course was the first non–North American club to achieve full certification with the Audubon Cooperative Sanctuary Program for Golf Courses.

Valderrama is named after an old Andalucian estate. The course was designed by Jones to international acclaim. "Faced with such beautiful land," the architect wrote, "all my instincts were to leave well alone, as far as possible."

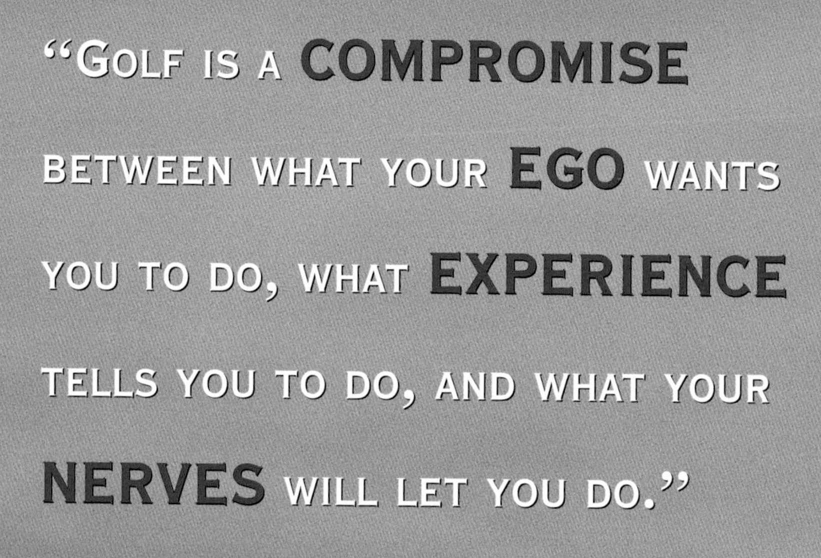

"Golf is a **compromise** between what your **ego** wants you to do, what **experience** tells you to do, and what your **nerves** will let you do."

—Bruce Crampton

Arnold Palmer: The Man, The Beverage

Years ago, so the story goes, Arnold Palmer began ordering a half-and-half mix of lemonade and iced tea in restaurants. According to the legendary golfer, the servers started referring to the beverage as an "Arnold Palmer," and the name stuck. One company has gone so far as to market an officially licensed version of the drink in bottles and cans.

Best Women's Majors

1954
U.S. Women's Open: Comeback from Cancer

In April 1953, Babe Zaharias underwent cancer surgery. Her doctor said she might not return to championship golf, but he underestimated her. She won the next year's U.S. Women's Open by 12 strokes. "When I was in the hospital, I prayed that I could play again," she said. "Now I'm happy because I can tell people not to be afraid of cancer."

1961
U.S. Women's Open: The Wright Way

Mickey Wright came into her own in 1961, the first of four straight years in which she captured at least ten LPGA Tour victories. She took control on the 36-hole final day of the Open at Baltusrol Golf Club's Lower Course in New Jersey with stunning rounds of 69 and 72 for a six-stroke victory.

1967
LPGA Championship: Whitworth's Bomb

Kathy Whitworth, who had never won the LPGA Championship or U.S. Women's Open, led wire-to-wire at the 1967 LPGA, but it was a nail-biter all the way. Tied with Shirley Englehorn before the final hole, Whitworth left herself a 50-foot birdie putt, which she rolled into the cup. Minutes later, Englehorn missed from 60 feet, and Whitworth had the major triumph she sought.

1997
U.S. Women's Open: The Spoiler ▶

At age 40, Nancy Lopez, one of the best players in LPGA history, still

hadn't claimed the biggest women's title. The first player ever to shoot in the 60s in all four rounds of a U.S. Women's Open with scores of 69–68–69–69, she lost to 35-year-old Briton Alison Nicholas, who shot a championship-record 10-under-par to nip Lopez by one.

1998 U.S. Women's Open: Kids' Stuff

An 18-hole playoff between 20-year-old Se Ri Pak and Jenny Chuasiriporn, who turned 21 during the tournament, would result in the youngest U.S. Women's Open champion ever. Tied heading to the 18th playoff hole, Pak drove into a hazard. That barely slowed her down. Shedding her shoes, she played the ball from the long grass on the bank to bogey the hole. Chuasiriporn three-putted, sending the championship into sudden-death. Pak ended the drama by birdieing the 20th hole.

Hold Her Gently

There have been many metaphors for how gently a golf club should be held, how light the pressure should be on the handle. For example, hold it as if it were an overripe tomato, or a balloon you don't want to pop. But Jimmy Demaret, who wore extremely colorful clothes to match his sunny personality and sensual nature, had the most memorable: "Hold the club as though it were the girl you want to marry."

Snead Wins the British but Loses Money

Sam Snead's powerfully smooth swing led him to a victory in the 1946 British Open, held for the first time since 1939. Snead was one of the few Americans to compete in the British, making the trip at the urging of his equipment company. Although he won the $600 first prize, Snead claimed the trip cost him $1,000.

Raymond Floyd

Raymond Floyd's father was career Army, and Floyd's march on the golf course mirrors his being raised on military bases—his back absolutely straight and his head high at attention.

Raymond's carriage may be responsible for his golf swing. It has been likened to the construct of a football linebacker, or perhaps a windmill with a screw or two loose. The club goes back sharply to the inside with a dip of his left shoulder, then is raised seemingly straight up to the completion of the backswing. The zigzag route is pretty much repeated going back to impact.

Floyd has said that his first 12 years as a touring pro, beginning in 1963, were "just a means to an end," a way to make money for wine, women, and song. He was also a notorious high-stakes gambler on his golf game. The early-1970s consensus was that Floyd's talent was going to waste, even though he had won a PGA Championship (1969) and four other Tour events.

Then he met his wife, Maria, who had a more conventional set of values. Everything was turned around. In 1975, after four years without a victory and with the first of his three children just born, Floyd won the Kemper Open. He followed that in 1976 with an astounding eight-shot victory in the Masters as well as a win in the World Open. From 1977 to 1992, he won 15 times, including the U.S. Open in 1986, becoming, at 43, the oldest winner of the national championship until that time.

Floyd was expected to be a terror on the Senior circuit, and he delivered by winning 13 events in his first four years after turning 50. He is one of just two golfers to win tournaments on the PGA Tour in four different decades. The only other golfer with such staying power? Sam Snead.

aureus

Chapter Six

Titanium Drivers and Graphite Shafts:

Modern Golf

A new generation of competitors steps forward as the game closes out one century and enters another.

Ireland's Darren Clarke tees off for the European team in the 2004 Ryder Cup.

Jack Nicklaus

Jack Nicklaus's first professional victory, at the 1962 U.S. Open at Oakmont Country Club near Pittsburgh, was over Arnold Palmer in a playoff. Palmer, at the height of his game, was incredibly popular. Nicklaus, overweight, had the air of a pampered country-club golfer.

Thus, when he defeated Palmer rather handily, not only outplaying but outhitting him off the tee, Nicklaus was treated with disdain. But eventually, he brought everyone to his side with consistently outstanding golf and an acute sense of fair play, a champion in every way.

After Nicklaus won his second Masters in 1965 at age 25, Bobby Jones remarked that Jack was playing a game "with which I am not familiar," undoubtedly referring to the height of Nicklaus's long iron shots. With an unusually high trajectory, the ball seemed to hang forever in the air before landing softly. It also carried astonishingly in its distance. Jones also had in mind Nicklaus's exceptional putting touch and a level of poise under pressure incredible for so young a man. What would make these attributes all the more exceptional was how long they persisted.

Nicklaus would go on to win a total of 73 tournaments on the PGA Tour, which included six Masters, four U.S. Opens, five PGA Championships, and three British Opens. With two U.S. Amateur titles, his 20 major titles are seven more than anyone else's.

Nicklaus's longevity is as impressive as his haul of tournament hardware. The youngest to ever win the Masters at 23 in 1963 (since surpassed), in 1986 he became, at 46, the oldest winner. From Ben Hogan to Tiger Woods, Nicklaus has competed against a Who's Who of golf greats. His designation as the greatest golfer in the history of the game can hardly be denied.

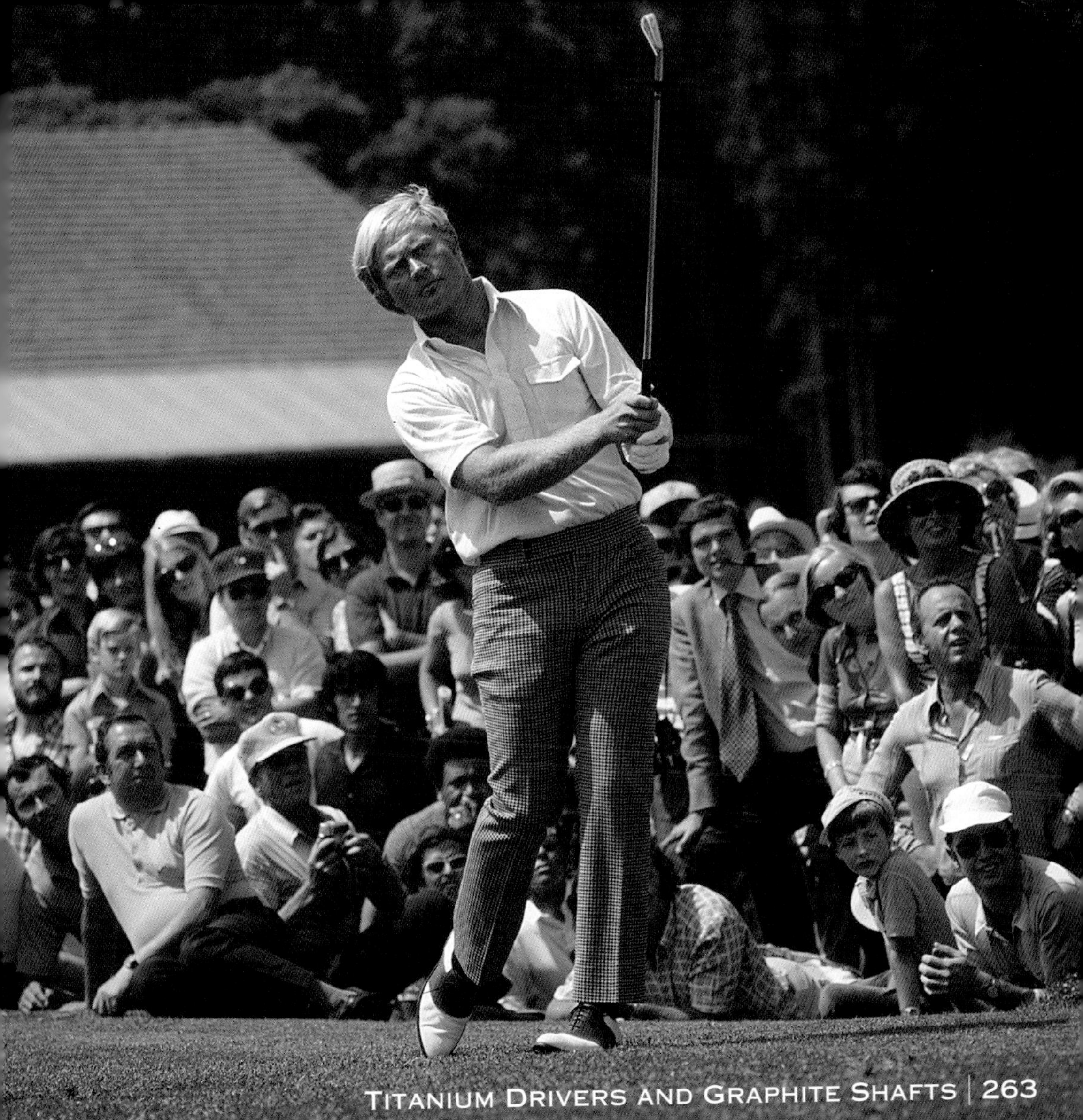

"Golf combines two favorite American pastimes: taking long walks and hitting things with a stick."

—P. J. O'Rourke, *Modern Manners*

"Your financial cost can best be figured when you realize that if you were to devote the same time and energy to business instead of golf, you would be a millionaire in approximately six weeks."

—Buddy Hackett

The most dominating performance in a dominant year for Tiger Woods came in the U.S. Open at Pebble Beach. Woods won the last three majors of the year, adding a rout at the British Open and a nail-biter at the PGA Championship.

Tiger Shoots 53-Under in Majors, Wins Three

No person has ever played better golf than Tiger Woods did in 2000. The U.S. Open at Pebble Beach provided the most dramatic example. Woods posted the largest victory margin in major championship golf history—15 strokes. He was 12-under-par, the first player to finish a U.S. Open in double digits under par.

Next on the agenda was the British Open at St. Andrews. Woods had won each of the other three majors and had a chance to become the youngest player—and fifth overall—to achieve the career Grand Slam. There was never a doubt, as Woods broke the British Open under-par record at 19-under and won by eight strokes.

At the PGA Championship, Woods finally received some competition but prevailed in one of the most thrilling final-round shootouts the game has ever seen. When unheralded Bob May shot a 31 on the back nine at Valhalla, Woods matched it. He then birdied the first hole of a three-hole playoff to take control, becoming the only player besides Ben Hogan in 1953 to claim three professional majors in a year. Woods and May set a championship record of 18-under for 72 holes, giving Woods the under-par record at all four major championships (he set the Masters mark in 1997).

Woods was a cumulative 53-under-par for the majors, 25 strokes better than the next best in history. There was more to Woods's year than the majors. He won nine of the 20 events he entered, the second-best percentage in modern history to Byron Nelson's 18 of 30 in 1945. Woods's scoring average for the year of 68.17 topped Nelson's 68.33 in 1945. He earned $9,188,321, nearly double that of runner-up Phil Mickelson.

"PRESSURE IS PLAYING FOR TEN DOLLARS WHEN YOU'VE ONLY GOT FIVE IN YOUR POCKET."

—LEE TREVINO

The Stadium Course Opens at PGA West

Pete Dye, asked by the Landmark Land Company to design the toughest course in the world, obliged with the Stadium Course at PGA West in La Quinta, California. Dye incorporated small greens and pot bunkers into this brutally tough desert track. The course opened in 1986 and played host to the Skins Game from 1986 to 1991.

Greg Norman

Throughout his career, Greg Norman has been an enigma. Winner of nearly 90 tournaments worldwide and more than $13 million in PGA Tour prize money, he may still go down in the game's annals for how many major championships he lost.

In 1986, Norman held the lead in all four of the majors going into the final round of play, yet he won just the British Open. He is the only golfer in history to have lost a playoff for each of the majors (1984 U.S. Open, 1987 Masters, 1989 British Open, 1993 PGA). In the 1996 Masters, his collapse in the final round was one of the most astonishing and perplexing of them all. He tied the course record with 63 in the first round, then—with a six-shot lead going into the final round—shot a 78 to finish second, five shots behind Nick Faldo. It was the largest lead ever blown in the last round of a major championship.

Norman, from Queensland, Australia, turned pro in 1976 and began competing on the Australian Tour. He then moved to the international circuits. From 1977 through 1982, "The Shark" won at least one tournament every year, including the Australian Open, Australian Masters, French Open, and Dunlop Masters.

Throughout his career, Norman either won big, dominating the field, or let others catch him with his mediocre-to-poor play. Still, his overall record is remarkable. Over 14 seasons through 1997 on the U.S. Tour, he posted 116 top-10 finishes, including 20 victories, and won the Vardon Trophy for low scoring average three times. The money followed. He set a PGA Tour season record in 1995 for money won with $1,654,959 and soared to No. 1 on the money list for the third time despite playing a limited schedule.

"Thinking must be the hardest thing to do in golf, because we do so little of it."

—Harvey Penick

"All my life I wanted to play golf like Jack Nicklaus, and now I do."

—Paul Harvey, after Nicklaus shot an 83 in a tournament

The $10-Million Man

Vijay Singh had a stellar year in 2004, becoming the first professional golfer to win more than $10 million in a single season. His final total was $10,905,166, almost doubling runner-up Ernie Els's winnings of $5,787,225. On the way to that landmark, Singh captured nine PGA Tour victories, including the PGA Championship. To cap off his championship season, Singh was voted PGA Tour Player of the Year, breaking Tiger Woods's five-year hold on the title.

"Baseball players quit playing and they take up golf. Basketball players quit, take up golf. Football players quit, take up golf. What are we supposed to take up when we quit?"

—George Archer

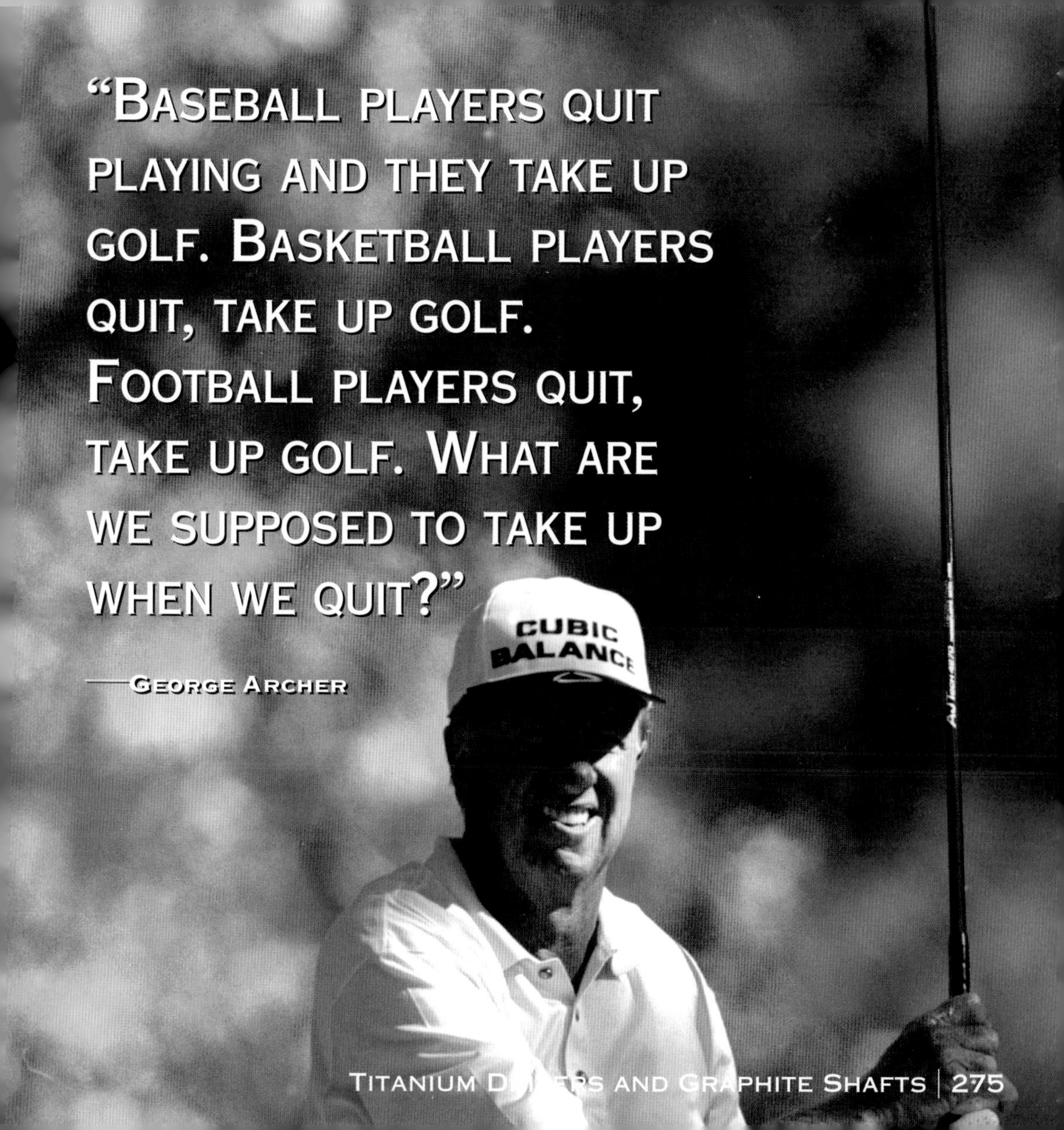

Watson Tops Nicklaus; A New King Is Crowned

In the 1960s, Jack Nicklaus—ten years younger than Arnold Palmer—succeeded Arnie as golf's top player. In the 1970s, Tom Watson, nearly ten years younger than Nicklaus, became the next superstar.

To start the 1977 season, Watson won the Bing Crosby National Pro-Am and the Andy Williams San Diego Open. At the Masters at Augusta National, he challenged Nicklaus face-to-face. Watson was the third-round leader at Augusta, and even though Nicklaus buried six birdies on the first 13 holes on Sunday, Watson stayed with him. Nicklaus finished the fourth round with a 66, but Watson's 67 was good enough to defeat Nicklaus by two strokes.

The head-on duel was renewed at the British Open at Turnberry. In the pleasant weather of the first three rounds, Nicklaus and Watson each shot 68–70–65, and the two entered the final round three strokes ahead of the field. That round, with Nicklaus and Watson paired together, was more of a match-play than a stroke-play finale. Nicklaus led much of the way, but Watson claimed the lead on the 17th and, with a birdie on the 18th, defeated Nicklaus for a second time that year.

By winning two majors face-to-face with the Golden Bear, Watson proved he could beat anybody. He also won the Western Open in the United States and became the year's leading money winner. He would lead the Tour in earnings from 1977 to 1980 and become golf's new and undisputed king.

This photo, taken at the 1977 Masters, reflects the changing of the guard on the PGA Tour. Watson (right) *won the Masters by two strokes over Nicklaus* (left), *then outlasted Jack in a classic final-round face-off at Turnberry for the British Open title. Watson, not Nicklaus, now reigned as golf's best player.*

Curtis Strange

Strange, who won back-to-back U.S. Open championships in 1988 and 1989, is the only player to achieve that feat in the last 50 years.

His outstanding amateur record included victories in the 1974 NCAA Championship, the 1973 Southeastern Amateur, the 1974 Western Amateur, the 1975 Eastern Amateur, and the 1975 and 1976 North and South Amateurs.

With winnings totaling more than $2 million, he led the PGA Tour in earnings in 1987 and 1988.

"The mystery of golf is that nobody can master it," Strange said. "You can shoot a good score today, but can you do it tomorrow?"

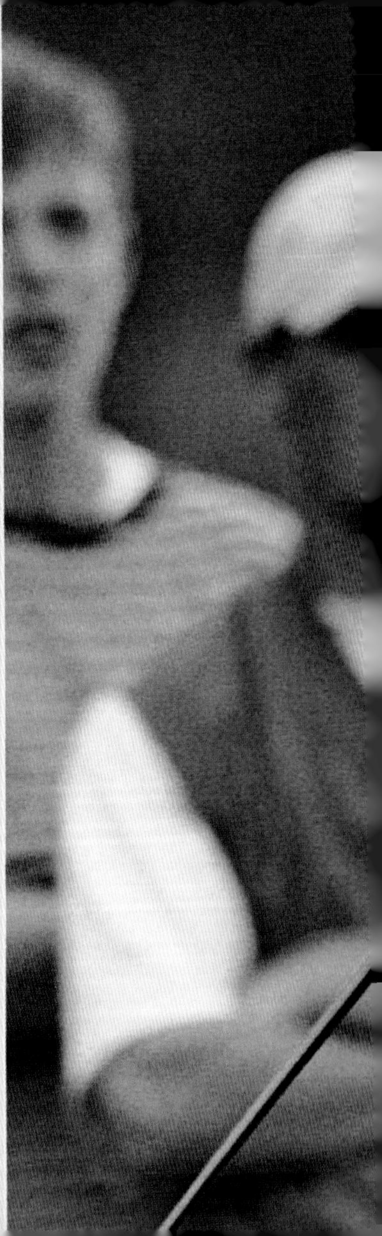

Titleist

"He wanted me to change my takeaway, my backswing, my downswing, and my follow-through. He said I could still play right-handed."

—Brad Bryant, on receiving instruction from David Leadbetter

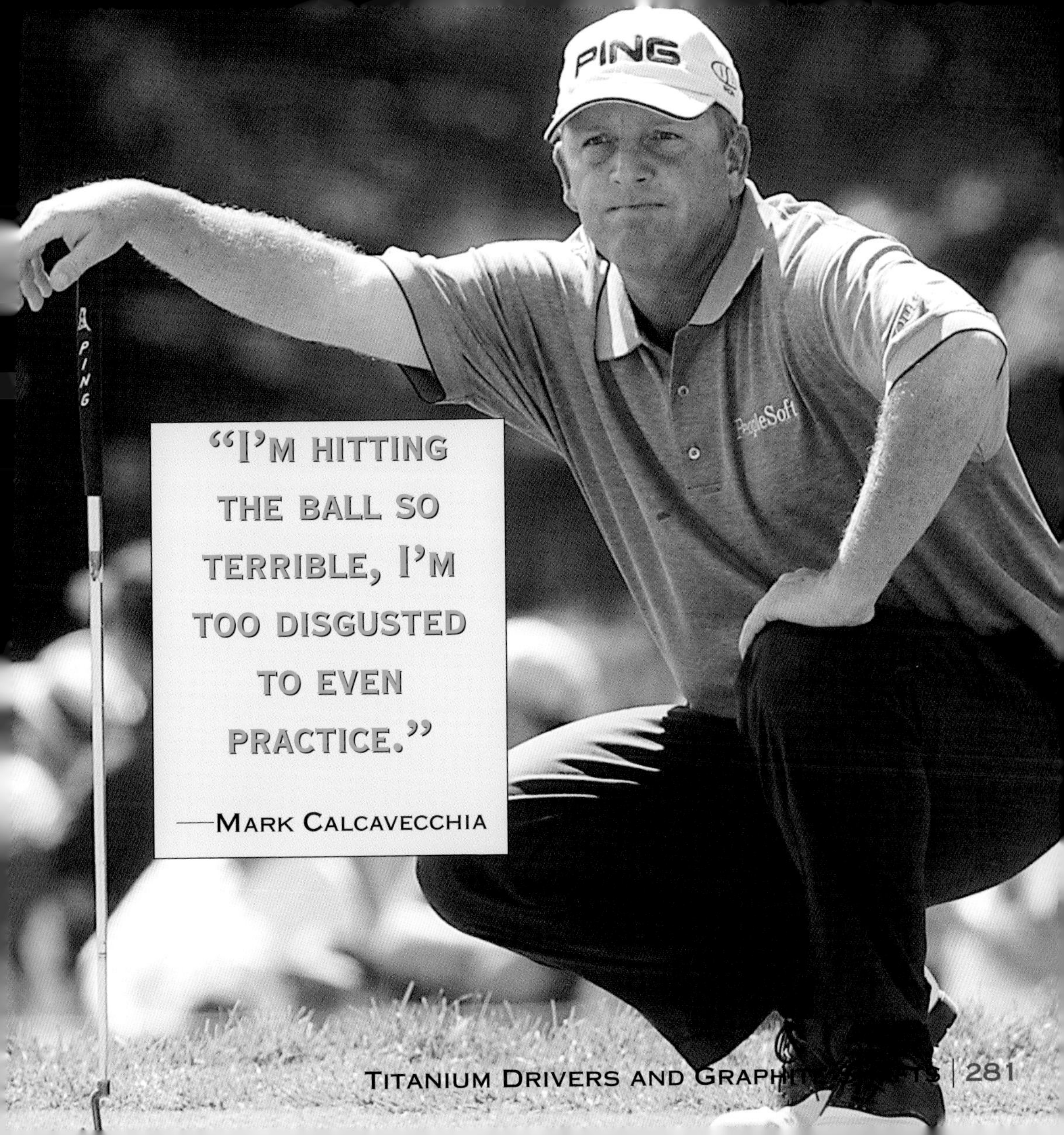
PING
PING
PeopleSoft
"I'M HITTING THE BALL SO TERRIBLE, I'M TOO DISGUSTED TO EVEN PRACTICE."
—MARK CALCAVECCHIA

Miller Cashes In with Eight Tour Wins

Winning at least one major championship is generally considered the foundation for winning Player of the Year. But Johnny Miller proved that common wisdom false when he was crowned the PGA Tour's top player in 1974 after winning eight non-major PGA Tour events and setting a record for the most money won in a season.

Miller's 1974 season started oddly. The first tournament was the Bing Crosby National Pro-Am. Rain and hail bombed Pebble Beach, and after three rounds Miller had a four-stroke lead. When more rain caused the final round to be canceled, he was declared the winner. He won again at the Phoenix Open and made it three in a row by beating Ben Crenshaw at the Dean Martin Tucson Open. Through these tournaments, Miller was 37-under-par. He finished fourth at the Bob Hope Desert Classic and fifth at the Los Angeles Open, rolling up an amazing 24 consecutive rounds of par or less.

Miller's fourth victory was at the Sea Pines Heritage Classic at Hilton Head, South Carolina, but he tied for 15th at the Masters. Two weeks later, he won the Tournament of Champions and in late August won the Westchester Classic in New York by shooting 19-under-par.

A $60,000 first-place check at the World Open at Pinehurst put him close to Jack Nicklaus's money-winning record. Miller went home to Napa Valley to play in the Kaiser International at Silverado Country Club, a course where he never did well despite living next to the 8th hole. Yet he broke 70 in all four rounds to win $30,000 and break Nicklaus's record. His season-ending total of $353,021.59 remained the Tour's highest until 1978.

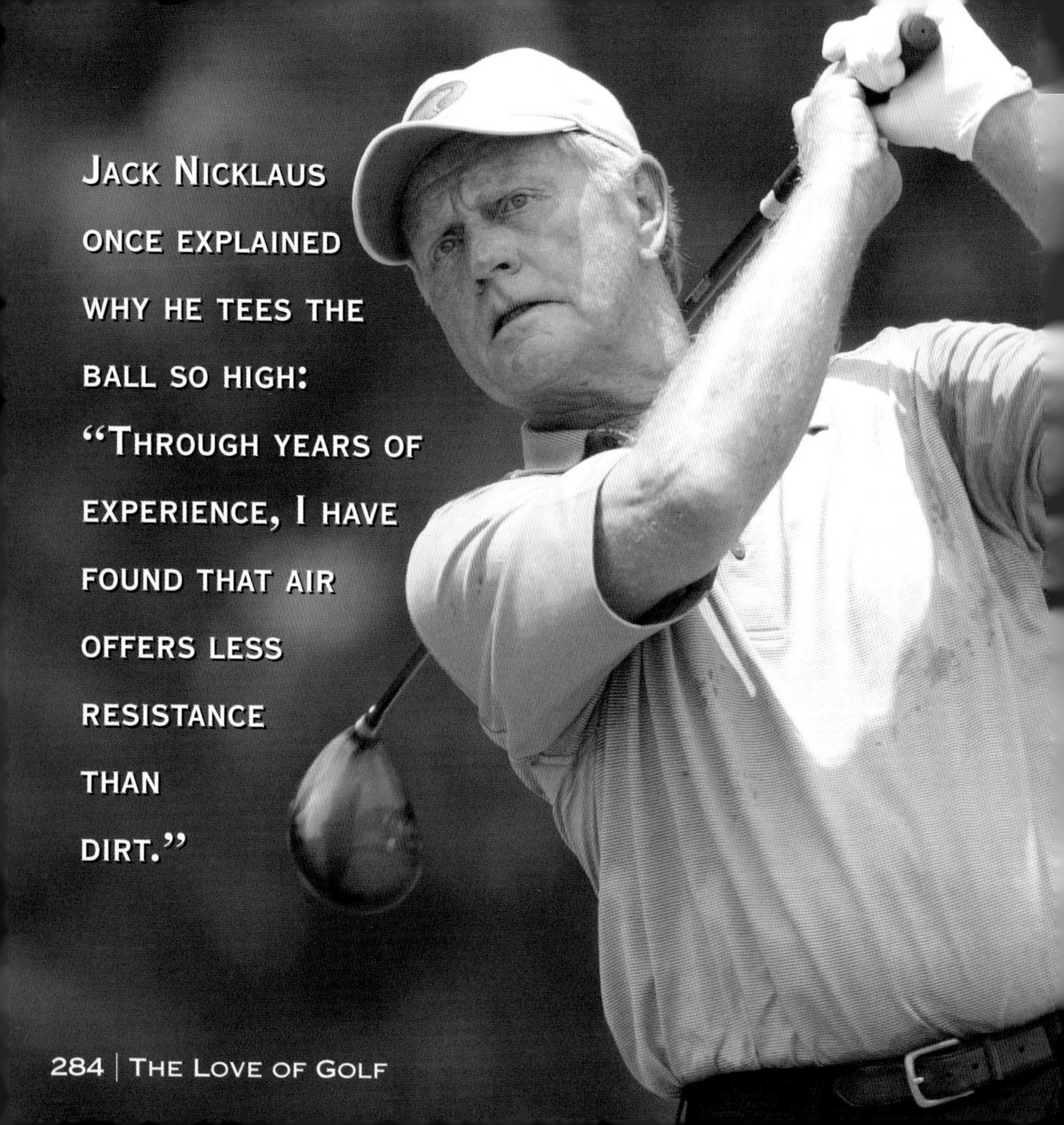

Jack Nicklaus once explained why he tees the ball so high: "Through years of experience, I have found that air offers less resistance than dirt."

"The person I fear most in the last two rounds is myself."

—Tom Watson

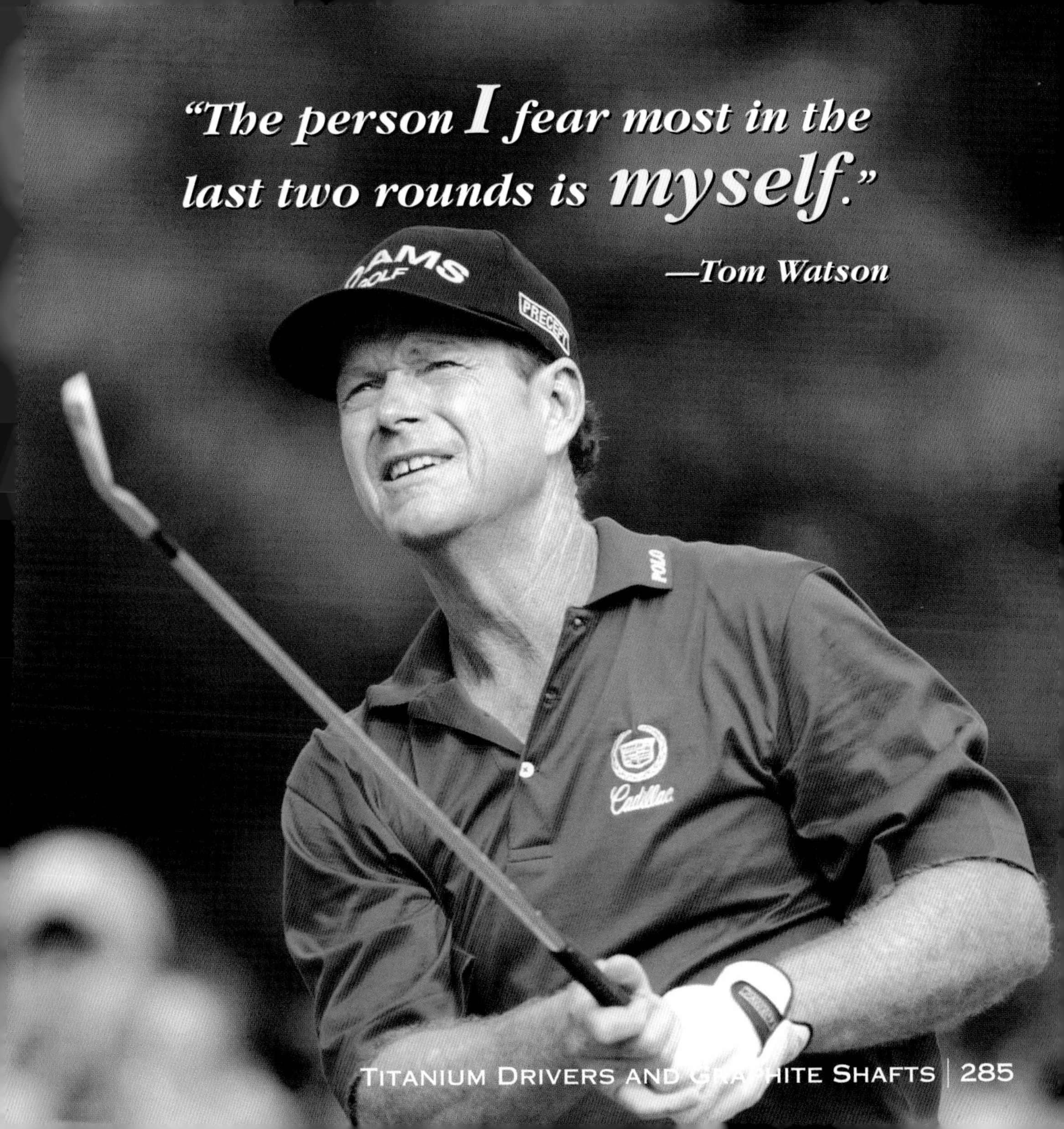

Rookie Lopez Racks Up Five Wins in a Row

A rookie year is always tough. Few rookies even win a tournament, and when one does, he or she is likely to be named Rookie of the Year. That's not what happened in 1978, when Nancy Lopez, a 21-year-old rookie from New Mexico, turned pro.

Lopez was Rookie of the Year, but that was the least of her achievements. She won an unbelievable nine LPGA Tour events including the LPGA Championship, which was part of five consecutive wins. She was also named Player of the Year and was the LPGA's leading money winner. No rookie, not even Jack Nicklaus or Tiger Woods, burst onto the scene like Lopez did.

Lopez's sensational amateur career made her a heralded rookie. In 1969 at age 12, she won the New Mexico State Amateur. And in 1975, she finished second in the U.S. Women's Open—as an 18-year-old.

For all intents and purposes, Lopez wrapped up the 1978 Rookie of the Year Award by March. On February 26, she won the Bent Tree Classic, then the next event, the Sunstar Classic. Two months later, she began the hottest winning streak in LPGA Tour history. Starting in May, she won the Baltimore Classic, Coca-Cola Classic, and Golden Lights Championship in successive weeks.

After taking a week off, Lopez captured the LPGA Championship for her first major. By winning the Bankers Trust Classic the following week, she had won five tournaments in six weeks.

Finishing the year with two more victories to win $189,813 gave Lopez another LPGA record. She became a household name. Shrugging off the sophomore slump in 1979, she won eight more events, giving her 17 before age 22. From 1980 to 1997, she won 31 more LPGA Tour events.

Lopez, pictured early in her career, joined the LPGA Tour midway through 1977 and won 17 of the first 50 tournaments in which she played.

TPC at Sawgrass

When Jerry Pate won the first Players Championship played at TPC Sawgrass in 1982, he took a celebratory plunge into the lake bordering the 18th green. He grabbed designer Pete Dye and PGA Tour Commissioner Deane Beman, who contributed to the design, and tossed them in as well. Tour pros chuckled in delight as the designers splashed into the water like so many of their errant shots.

The Stadium Course, with an island green on its signature 17th hole, was designed with outrageously small landing areas, enormous waste bunkers, tiny yet wildly undulating greens, tight tree-lined fairways, and water on every hole.

"This is Star Wars golf, created by Darth Vader," said Ben Crenshaw. "They messed up a perfectly good swamp," offered golfer J. C. Snead. He was referring to the 415-acre site, which the PGA Tour purchased for $1 in 1978 and turned into its worldwide headquarters. Snead also offered the opinion, "This course is 90 percent horse manure and 10 percent luck."

The Stadium Course's 17th hole is the most famous island hole in the world. The 132-yard par-3 has robbed many a pro golfer of his chance at winning the annual PGA Tour event held at the course.

PLAYERS

Aoki's Fortune Cookie

During the evening before the final round of the 1983 Buick Open, Japanese professional Isao Aoki decided to have Chinese food for dinner. When he finished the meal, he opened his fortune cookie, which had a message that read, "You will take a trip to the desert."

Sure enough, the next day Isao twice hit bunkers that resulted in bogeys, and he lost the tournament by one stroke.

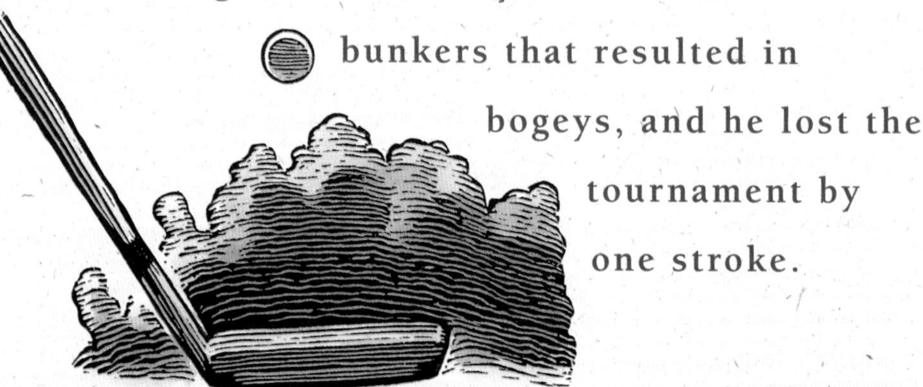

"Harbour Town is so tough, even your clubs get tired."

—Charles Price, *Inside Golf*

Nicklaus Wins the Greatest Masters of All

If you asked avid Masters fans, many would say the best Masters ever was the 1975 battle among Jack Nicklaus, Tom Weiskopf, and Johnny Miller.

After starting with a 68 and a 67, Nicklaus seemed to have the Masters wrapped up going into the third round. Nobody paid attention to Miller, who opened with a 75, until they looked at the leaderboard and noticed Johnny ringing up birdie after birdie. He birdied six holes in a row and cruised in with a 65. Weiskopf shot a 66, which, after Nicklaus chugged in with a 73, took the lead.

The next day was even more exciting. By the time they got to the back nine, Nicklaus and Weiskopf were tied for the lead, and Miller was right behind. Weiskopf bogied 16, right after Nicklaus holed a 40-foot birdie putt on the same hole to regain a tie. Miller birdied 17 to tie Weiskopf. Heading to the final hole, the two were one behind Nicklaus.

Both Miller and Weiskopf hit perfect tee shots on 18, and Miller hit his second shot 15 feet from the cup. Weiskopf followed with a second shot 8 feet from the cup. If either could make his birdie putt, he would meet Nicklaus in a playoff. Miller lined up the putt and seemed to hit it perfectly... yet the ball curled left just before reaching the hole. Weiskopf's putt rolled to the right.

Nicklaus claimed his fifth career Masters. Weiskopf was really disappointed. "How do you describe pain?" he asked the press. Miller told the media, "I'm not upset. I'm funny this way. I don't get down on myself when I don't win. I gave it my best, and 66 and 65 are not too shabby."

Nick Faldo

Nick Faldo's game was in the Ben Hogan mold, a paragon of consistency derived from solid and well-understood swing fundamentals combined with unassailable concentration and an unquenchable thirst for practice. Born in Hertfordshire, England, Faldo had success early on playing the European PGA Tour, but he discerned that to go to the very top, he would have to make major changes in his swing. Working with South African teaching professional David Leadbetter, Faldo completely revamped his technique. It took a full two years to bring the changes up to speed, and then everything fell into place. In 1987, Faldo won the British Open, making 18 pars in the final round to catch and pass a faltering Paul Azinger.

Faldo's star had now completely cleared the horizon, and his accomplishments began to multiply. In 1988, he won twice in Europe and lost in a playoff with Curtis Strange for the U.S. Open. Then in 1989, he captured his second major title, the Masters, after a playoff with Scott Hoch. He won four other events that year on the European Tour. In 1990, Faldo again won the Masters, and again in a playoff (with Raymond Floyd), to become only the second successful defender of that much-prized title. That same year, he won his second British Open crown. He won his national championship a third time in 1992.

For all his success over a ten-year stretch, Faldo went back to his drawing board for swing and playing adjustments. It worked. In 1995, he started to play the U.S. Tour regularly and won the Doral-Ryder Open. Then in 1996, he won his third Masters.

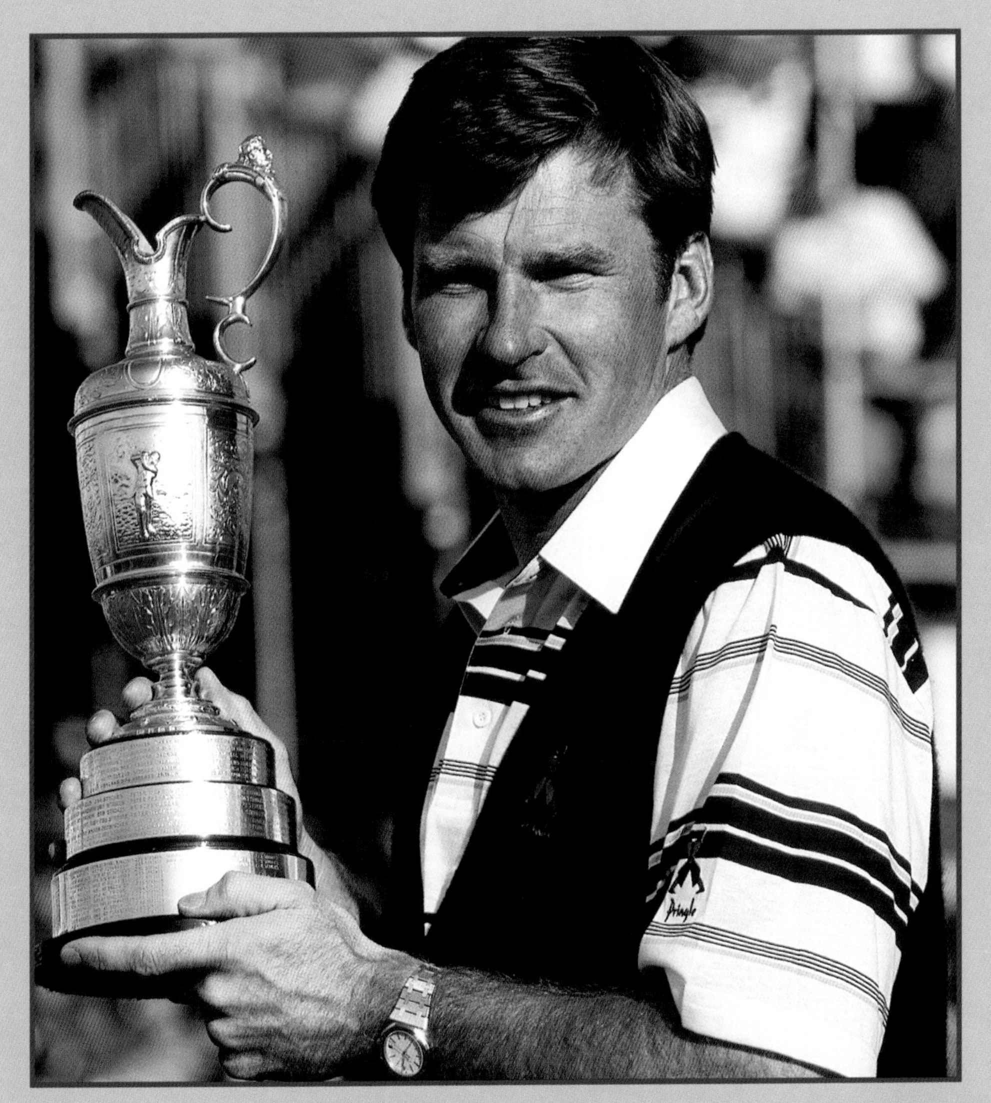
Pringle

Player Edges Three by a Stroke in Masters

Gary Player triumphed at the 1978 Masters, where at age 42, he became the oldest champion to don the green jacket until that time. After three rounds, Player had been down seven strokes, but he closed 34–30—64 to win by a stroke over Hubert Green, Rod Funseth, and Tom Watson. Watson could have tied with a par on 18, but he bogied.

Irwin Streaks to Nine Senior Victories

Hale Irwin dominated 1997's Senior Tour like nobody had since Lee Trevino seven years earlier. Frustrated with two wins and seven second-place finishes in 1996, Irwin regained his winning ways in 1997 with nine victories. His biggest triumph came by 12 strokes at the PGA Seniors' Championship. Through 2004, he'd racked up a record 40 Senior Tour wins.

Wow! Unknown Daly Booms His Way to PGA Title

Never has a golf hero been born so quickly as John Daly at the 1991 PGA Championship. Until then, only a few avid golf observers knew that the 25-year-old was the longest hitter on the PGA Tour and had posted a couple of top-10 finishes in his rookie season. But before it was over, he was a hero for the masses.

The making of a legend, appropriately, began with a story straight out of a Hollywood script. Daly, the ninth alternate based on his money earnings for the year, was unlikely to make the field at Crooked Stick Golf Club in Carmel, Indiana. By Tuesday, however, five players had withdrawn. Three alternates declined to travel to Indiana on the chance another player would drop out. But Daly was willing to go. He hopped into his car at 5:00 P.M. Wednesday for the 7½-hour drive from his Memphis home. When he arrived in Carmel, Daly received a message that he was in. Nick Price had withdrawn when he got word

that his wife was about to deliver their first child.

Daly began to gain attention with a 67 in the second round to take the lead. By the weekend, fans were flocking to see this swashbuckling blond kid crush the ball. And Daly, an engaging, friendly sort, fed on the crowd's energy.

His third-round 69 to take a three-stroke lead was an impressive display, marred only by a double bogey on the 8th hole, where he hit a sand wedge an impossible 150 yards, ending up in the water over the green. He grabbed a five-stroke lead midway through the back nine, and a final-round 71 enabled him to win by three.

Tom Watson

Only one golfer ever came close to challenging Jack Nicklaus as golf's most dominant player. From 1974 to 1984, Tom Watson won eight major championships and 36 tournaments overall on the PGA Tour.

Watson joined the PGA Tour in 1971 and broke through in 1975 to win the British Open, a tournament he would win five times (1975, 1977, 1980, 1982, and 1983), one less than Harry Vardon's six triumphs. Only one other player, Peter Thomson, has won the honored title five times in the modern era.

In the 1977 British Open at Turnberry, Scotland, Watson's victory over Nicklaus was the most dynamic one-on-one confrontation in golf history. Each competitor shot 68–70 in rounds one and two, then playing together, they matched 65s in round three. Watson led the final round by a stroke going to the last hole. He drove perfectly into the fairway. Nicklaus drove into deep gorse. Watson played an 8-iron approach to within 30 inches of the hole. Miraculously, Nicklaus freed his ball from the thicket, the ball finishing 32 feet from the cup. He then ran the putt in for a round of 66, beating the British Open 72-hole scoring record by seven shots—but he still lost. Watson holed for a 65.

Watson also won two Masters, both in duels with Nicklaus. And in 1982 at Pebble Beach, it appeared Nicklaus would win his fifth U.S. Open. But, in an unforgettable moment, Watson chipped in from a heavy lie in the fringe off the 17th green for a birdie-2. This gave him a one-shot lead, which he maintained.

Watson continued his powerful, well-thought-out golf through 1984, when he won three times on the PGA Tour, but then his game went into a steep decline. Perhaps he needed Nicklaus to inspire him, but by that time Jack was finally winding down his own competitive career.

"Charisma," Watson said, "is winning major championships."

Mize Holes Chip Shot, Breaks Norman's Heart

Larry Mize leaps toward the heavens after winning the 1987 Masters. Mize won on the second hole of sudden-death, the 11th at Augusta National. He was 45 yards from the pin and hoping just to get up and down for a par. But miraculously, he pulled out his sand wedge and chipped it in, sending Greg Norman to another agonizing defeat.

Tway Holes Out from Bunker to Claim PGA

Bob Tway is rightfully excited after sinking an incredible bunker shot on the 72nd hole to take the 1986 PGA Championship away from previous leader Greg Norman. At the halfway point, Tway was nine strokes off the lead. Despite a third-round 64, he trailed Norman by four strokes. But in the final round, Tway outscored Norman 70–76.

Muirfield Village

Muirfield Village Golf Club, named after the legendary Scottish club, was one of Jack Nicklaus's first designs. It is considered by many to be his best.

Maybe it's because Muirfield Village is located in Dublin, Ohio, a suburb of Columbus, Nicklaus's hometown. Maybe it's because he worked with noted architect Desmond Muirhead or because the rolling hills are perfectly suited to a golf course. Whatever the reason, at No. 18 among America's 100 Greatest Courses, Muirfield Village is the highest-ranked Nicklaus layout in *Golf Digest*'s biannual survey of the nation's best courses.

Course conditioning and environmental sensitivity are two of the hallmarks of the 220-acre course. It is also home to all types of wildlife,

including Canada geese, deer, minks, blue herons, and red-tailed hawks.

Then there's the layout itself. The 7,265-yard track has 74 bunkers and water hazards on 12 holes. The long, straight hitter with a bit of a fade, much like Nicklaus himself, can do well here. Those who miss greens, however, will often have trouble.

The 363-yard 14th is considered one of the best par-4s in the country, with trees on either side of the landing area and a narrow brook across the fairway roughly 80 yards short of the green. The 478-yard 17th forces golfers to think on their feet. A huge fairway bunker looms on the left side, to which the precise driver wants to stay as close as possible to set up a prime approach to the green.

Muirfield Village was Nicklaus's dream course. It opened in 1974 with an exhibition match between Nicklaus and Tom Weiskopf. Jack's 6-under-par 66 held up as the course record until 1979.

Trevino Wins Three Big Ones in 21 Days

Even though Lee Trevino had won the 1968 U.S. Open, had captured four other PGA Tour events, and was 1970's leading money winner, his oddball golf swing and clowning on the golf course didn't earn him much respect. Early in 1971, Jack Nicklaus told him that if he took it seriously, he could be one of golf's all-time greats.

In the U.S. Open, Nicklaus would regret his advice. Merion Golf Club's tight fairways and tricky greens were made to order for Trevino's game, and Super Mex roared home in the final round with a back-nine 33 to tie Nicklaus at even-par 280.

Trevino greeted the Golden Bear at the next day's playoff by tossing a rubber snake at him, showing that he could remain relaxed despite facing the game's greatest player in the country's biggest golf event. Relaxation worked—he posted a 68 to Nicklaus's 71, winning his second U.S. Open.

Trevino gained instant credibility, but events over the next three weeks lifted him to a new level. At the Canadian Open at Montreal's Richelieu Valley Country Club, Trevino trailed Art Wall by two shots going into the final round. Super Mex rallied with three birdies on the back nine to force a playoff. He holed an 18-footer for a birdie on the first playoff hole, becoming the first golfer since Tommy Armour in 1927 to win the U.S. and Canadian Opens in the same year.

But his hot streak wasn't over. After three rounds at the British Open at Royal Birkdale, he held a one-shot lead over Briton Tony Jacklin and Taiwanese golfer Lu Liang Huan. His lead held, and Trevino won his third national championship in 21 days.

That afternoon, when defending champion Nicklaus gave Trevino the claret jug, he jokingly told the crowd, "I should have kept my mouth shut."

"My rule of thumb is to subtract 15 percent and then guess."

—Davis Love III, on club selection at mile-high Castle Pines

Two Strokes for Sharing

Paired with Lee Trevino during the final round of the 1980 Tournament of Champions at La Costa Resort, Tom Watson was cruising through his round as they approached the next tee. Trevino was not on his game.

Wanting to help his friend, Watson told Trevino he was playing the ball too far forward in his stance. The comment went out over national television, and a viewer called La Costa. By the time Tom got to the scorer's tent, PGA Tour director Jack Tuthill caught up with him, inquiring about the incident. Watson readily admitted he had given advice and was promptly assessed a two-stroke penalty. Had Tom signed the card before the discussion with Tuthill, he could have been disqualified. He still won the tournament by three strokes. Ironically, Watson had just authored a book on the rules of golf for the USGA.

Nancy Lopez

Nancy Lopez's streak of five wins in her rookie year immediately hoisted her, and the LPGA, into the spotlight of big-time golf. It didn't hurt that she also had one of the most beautiful smiles in sports, one that reflected the natural warmth of her character.

Nancy's family in Roswell, New Mexico, had no money for lessons, so she was largely self-taught. At 12, she won the New Mexico Women's Amateur championship. Quickly deemed a golfing prodigy, Nancy was invited to play and practice as often as she liked at Roswell country clubs. Lopez won the U.S. Girls' Junior championship in 1972 and 1974 and the Mexican Women's Amateur in 1975. That same year, she entered her first U.S. Women's Open and tied for second.

In addition to these accomplishments, Lopez—the wife of former baseball star Ray Knight—found the time and energy to become a mother of three children and to raise them conscientiously. Her first daughter was born in 1983, her second in 1986. Within those years and up to 1991, when she gave birth to her third daughter (and won a tournament while pregnant), Lopez won 19 tournaments, earned more than $2 million in prize money, and had a stroke average of just over 71.

She continued to play a full schedule of tournaments throughout the 1990s, retiring after 2002. In the 1992 Rail Charity Classic, she tied her career-low score, a 64, in the final round to take the title. In 1997, she won her 48th and final official LPGA tournament, which ranks seventh all time. In 1987, she was inducted into the LPGA Hall of Fame.

n the 1970s, the LPGA nged for a dynamic star to park interest in the sport. nter Lopez. As a rookie in 978, she graced the cover f Sports Illustrated.

The Grand Master Enjoys One Last Hurrah

Jack Nicklaus played his first Masters in 1959. Entering the 1986 Masters, he had won the tournament a record five times and established the 72-hole record of 271 in 1965. But never had he played a finer or more dramatic round at Augusta National than he did in 1986, at the age of 46, to claim his sixth green jacket.

It had been six years since Nicklaus had won a major, two since his last tournament win, and some wrote him off as a Masters contender. The Golden Bear went into Sunday four strokes off Greg Norman's lead. Through eight holes of the final round, Nicklaus was even par for the day and did not seem to be a major threat. But then lightning struck.

Nicklaus birdied the 9th hole, then played the back nine in 30 strokes, tying the tournament record (since broken). He birdied the 10th and 11th, bogied the 12th, and came back with a birdie at the 13th but still trailed Seve Ballesteros by four strokes. Nicklaus eagled the par-5 15th and nearly scored a hole-in-one on the par-3 16th before making a three-footer birdie.

Two-time Masters champion Ballesteros had grabbed the lead with eagles at the 8th and 13th holes, but, perhaps shaken by the roars greeting Nicklaus's heroics up ahead, faltered badly, bogeying the 15th. Suddenly, it was tied. Nicklaus had one more birdie on the 17th. Ballesteros posted another bogey to knock himself out of it, but the game was by no means over. Nicklaus parred the 18th to finish the tournament at 9-under, with a finishing 65. Several players on the course still had a chance, but Nick Price, Norman, and Tom Kite weren't up to the task.

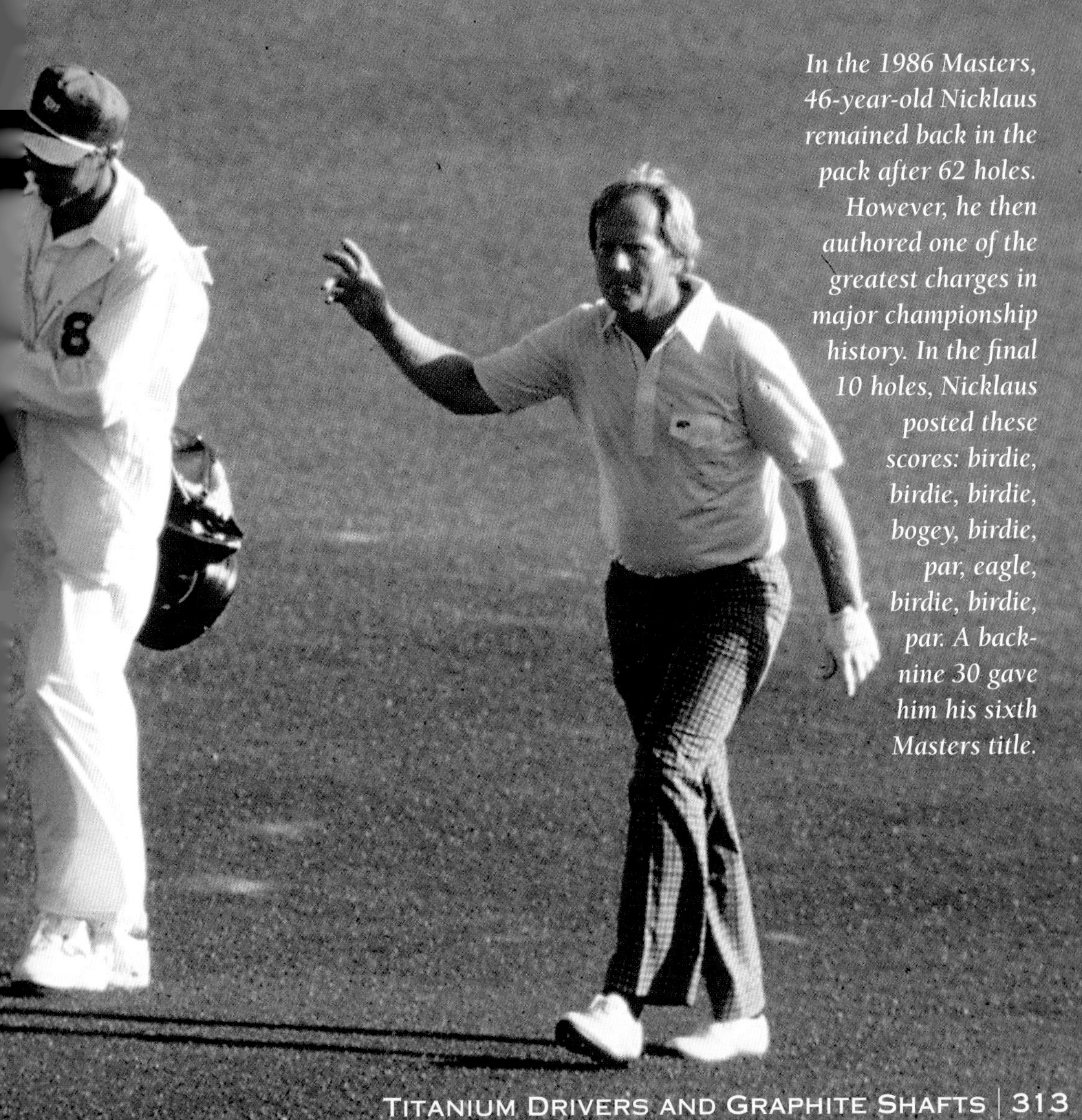

In the 1986 Masters, 46-year-old Nicklaus remained back in the pack after 62 holes. However, he then authored one of the greatest charges in major championship history. In the final 10 holes, Nicklaus posted these scores: birdie, birdie, birdie, bogey, birdie, par, eagle, birdie, birdie, par. A back-nine 30 gave him his sixth Masters title.

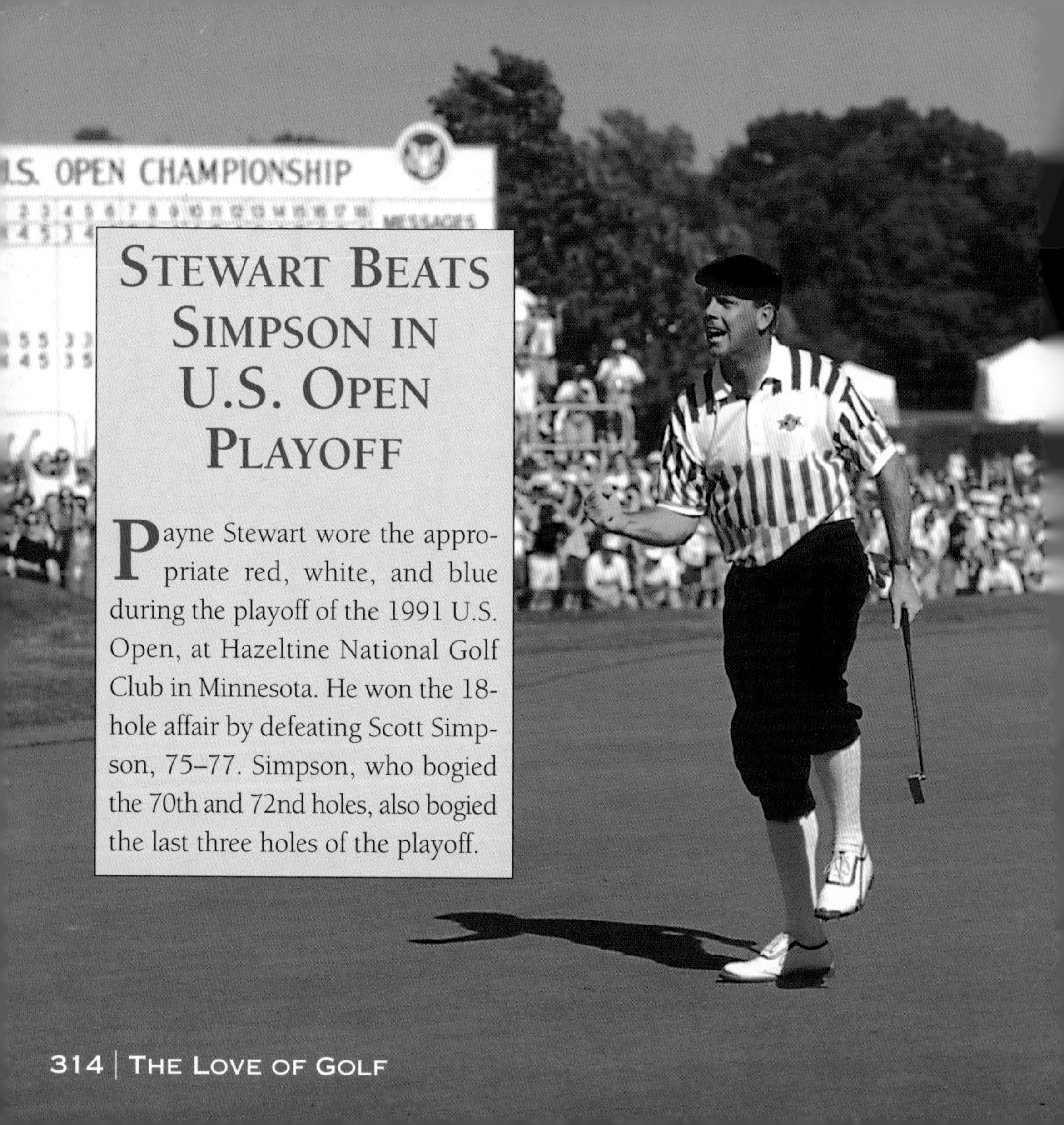

Stewart Beats Simpson in U.S. Open Playoff

Payne Stewart wore the appropriate red, white, and blue during the playoff of the 1991 U.S. Open, at Hazeltine National Golf Club in Minnesota. He won the 18-hole affair by defeating Scott Simpson, 75–77. Simpson, who bogied the 70th and 72nd holes, also bogied the last three holes of the playoff.

"My sole ambition in the game is to do well enough to give it up."

—David Feherty

Index

N

O

P

R

S

Picture credits:

Courtesy of the Amateur Athletic Foundation of Los Angeles: 61, 81, 93, 113, 182, 204, 219, 231, 247; **AP Wide World Photos:** 7, 8, 13, 16–17, 19, 23, 29, 31, 36–37, 42, 43, 44, 47, 51, 56, 57, 58, 62, 77, 79, 84, 85, 99, 103, 106, 109, 111, 112, 116, 124, 132, 137, 155, 160, 161, 172, 174, 178–179, 181, 183, 186, 189, 191, 194, 200, 203, 205, 206, 211, 222, 223, 226, 227, 233, 237, 239, 241, 266, 269, 277, 278–279, 292; **Getty Images:** 4–5, 15, 24, 40–41, 46, 48, 66, 67, 70, 73, 87, 96–97, 129, 131, 135, 142, 150, 153, 162, 163, 171, 184, 207, 232 (bottom), 257, 296; David Alexander, 52–53; Allsport, 117, 250–251; Allsport/Hulton Archive, 121; David Cannon, 152, 243, 260–261, 268, 295, 302, 303, 311, 313, 314; David Cannon/Allsport, 11, 193, 208–209; Stanley Chou, 271; Malcolm Clarke/Keystone, 287; Timothy A. Clary/AFP, 119; J.D. Cuban, 83; Stephen Dunn/Allsport, 125, 156; Jon Ferrey, 275; Jeff Gross, 285; Otto Greule Jr./Allsport, 228–229; Scott Halleran, 86, 274; Hulton Archive, 306; Keystone, 282; Ross Kinnaird, 123; Craig Lassig/AFP, 281; Andy Lyons, 249, 284, 297; Andy Lyons/Allsport, 235; Darren McNamara/Allsport, 199; Stephen Munday, 126–127, 168–169, 299; Gary Newkirk/Allsport, 102, 304–305; Steve Powell, 177; Steve Powell/Allsport, 148–149; Andrew Redington, 220–221; Jamie Squire, 288–289, 301; Time Life Pictures, 32, 60, 74, 80, 100–101, 105, 114–115, 118, 139, 140, 225; Stephen Wade/Allsport, 144; Todd Warshaw/Allsport, 255; **Glen Abbey Golf Course, Oakville, Ontario:** 212–213; **Inverness Club, Toledo, Ohio:** 91; **Life Touch Studios:** 94; **PIL Collection:** 75, 90, 95; **Popperfoto/Retrofile:** 68–69, 107, 145, 167; **SportsChrome:** 72, 88, 89, 232 (top), 259, 308, 309; **SuperStock:** 65, 263; **The Tufts Archives:** 159, 198; **Fred Vuich/*Golf Magazine*:** 26–27, 146–147.

Contributing Illustrators: Mark McIntosh, Keith Ward, John Zielinski.